Presented to:

_____

From:

_____

Date:

_____

"My father-in-law, Bishop Bill Hamon, has been in ministry for over 65 years and has experienced many challenging seasons, both personally and ministerially. In *Your Highest Calling*, he shares powerful keys for overcoming difficulties and living a life of success, fulfillment and victory. A must-read for every believer!"

Jane Hamon, co-apostle, Vision Church
at Christian International

"Dr. Bill Hamon offers powerful insight into God's highest calling for our lives while confronting the barriers that obstruct our path. A profound legacy message!"

Benny Hinn, pastor, Benny Hinn Ministries

"In a very real sense, this book will serve as a personal prophecy for each reader. It answers the question, What is God doing? Hamon explains both the highest and the lowest points of life. Courage and a new sense of purpose await behind each chapter heading. Enjoy the journey!"

Bishop Harry R. Jackson Jr., senior pastor,
Hope Christian Church, Beltsville, Maryland

"Bishop Bill Hamon is one of the wisest people I know. He has lived the message of this book. Bishop Hamon is one of the great Church historians of today, but he also understands building the character of Christ in God's people."

Cindy Jacobs, president and co-founder, Generals International

"Dr. Hamon's book, *Your Highest Calling*, defines the ultimate God-given destiny of mankind: to become like Jesus and co-labor with Him forever. Understanding this makes rejoicing in trials the only logical response, as the outcome is more glorious than we could have ever imagined. I highly recommend this book for every believer, young and old alike."

Bill Johnson, senior leader, Bethel Church, Redding, California;
author, *The Way of Life* and *Raising Giant-Killers*

"I have read every book written by Dr. Hamon. Each one is full of prophetic insight concerning the times and seasons of the Prophetic and Apostolic movements. In *Your Highest Calling*, he writes not only as a prophet and a teacher, but also as a Pentecostal theologian. This book brings the relationship between God and mankind to its highest level to fulfill the highest purpose unto God!"

Dr. John P. Kelly, international convenor,
International Coalition of Apostolic Leaders

"I honor my spiritual father, Bishop Hamon. As the father of the modern Prophetic movement and a pioneer in the restoration of the Church, he is mightily anointed to bring transformative revelation. His latest book, *Your Highest Calling*, reveals our supreme purpose in life and ministry: to become like Jesus."

Apostle Guillermo Maldonado, King Jesus
International Ministry

"It doesn't matter what the enemy has done to distort your identity in God. You can shake off the remnants of those tattered garments and be re-clothed! No matter what you go through, you can shout, 'But God!' He will show Himself faithful. He will restore, He will heal, and He will move you forward into new levels of prophetic fulfillment. *Your Highest Calling* will cause you to expect God to move on your behalf to accomplish His plan for you."

Dr. Chuck D. Pierce, president, Global Spheres
and Glory of Zion International Ministries

"Dr. Hamon's legacy of pioneering the restoration of prophets and prophetic ministry has been so significant and far-reaching that only heaven can measure its full impact. In the pages of *Your Highest Calling*, you can now learn and apply many of the principles and truths that have made Bill Hamon the general that he is. Do yourself—and those you are destined to touch—a favor. Read and digest this book!"

Dr. Dutch Sheets, president, Dutch Sheets Ministries

"I have loved and highly respected Bishop Bill Hamon since my initial meeting with him in 1987. He's down-to-earth, relational, fatherly and even fun. Yet great knowledge and wisdom continually gush out of this seemingly ordinary man. To me this book is the story of how he's come to be the great man of God that he is—a man conformed to the image of Christ! And he's shared the story with us so that we can also become conformed to the image of Christ!"

Barbara J. Yoder, lead apostle, Shekinah Regional Apostolic
Center and Breakthrough Apostolic Ministries Network

YOUR
HIGHEST
CALLING

DISCOVER THE SECRET PROCESSES THAT FULFILL YOUR DESTINY

DR. BILL HAMON

Chosen

a division of Baker Publishing Group
Minneapolis, Minnesota

© 2019 by Bill Hamon

Published by Chosen Books
11400 Hampshire Avenue South
Bloomington, Minnesota 55438
www.chosenbooks.com

Chosen Books is a division of
Baker Publishing Group, Grand Rapids, Michigan

Printed in the United States of America

ISBN 978-0-8007-9982-3

Library of Congress Cataloging-in-Publication Control Number: 2019946950

Cover design by LOOK Design Studio

19 20 21 22 23 24 25   7 6 5 4 3 2 1

This book is dedicated to my loving and faithful wife of 59 years. She and I went through many Processes of Conformity in our journey to fulfill God's predestined purpose of us being conformed to Christlikeness. One of my greatest trials was when God put me through a process of having to die to being an active ordained minister. God could not answer my questions and problems for He was my teacher giving me the test, and teachers cannot give you answers when you are taking their tests. But my wonderful wife continually encouraged and reassured me that I would yet fulfill my ministerial calling. She was faithful and true until she went home to be with the Lord September 22, 2014. Her reward will be great.

Contents

9

3. God's Highest Desire and Purpose in Creating Man   42

4. God's Inheritance in the Saints   65

5. The Higher the Calling, the Greater the Testing Process   76

Foreword

Standing on a North Miami Beach bridge with yachts passing by in the dark blue water, my husband presented me with diamond earrings. He wanted to renew our wedding vows. It was a grand good-bye as he set out on a month-long trip to Latin America on a special work assignment. That was the last time I ever saw him.

After a good-bye kiss, he promised to call when he landed. Several hours after my phone should have rung, there was no call. I did not think too much of it, since cell coverage was spotty in the region. The next morning, however, our two-year-old daughter started asking for Daddy, so I called again. No answer. Days went by, then weeks. I could not reach him. My concern was growing, and my baby was increasingly adamant about seeing Daddy.

After three weeks passed, a friend urged me to call the U.S. embassy to help find him. What I found out was shocking: He had never entered the country to which he told me he was headed.

With my investigative journalism skills, I tracked his location through news organizations. I was told what country he was in and given a phone number where I could reach him.

When I called the number, a Spanish-speaking man answered. I asked him to put my husband on the phone. The man on the other end insisted that my husband was divorced and engaged to marry his daughter.

That is how I found out my husband had abandoned me. It was a life-changing, mind-blowing, earth-shattering event—and it would not be the first one.

Within months, I was accused of a crime I did not commit and landed in jail, fighting for my freedom. After forty days, I was vindicated and released, but it cost me every penny I had. I came out of jail with a small child, no job, no home and no money.

Decades ago, when I was picking up the pieces of my broken life, I had no idea that God would use the devil's one-two punch to prepare me for my highest calling. I discovered that Romans 8:28 is true—God really does work all things for the good of those who love Him and are called according to His purpose. I also realized that what does not kill us really does make us stronger. I learned that the trying of my faith was working patience in me so I could walk in my destiny.

I endured several life-changing, mind-blowing, earth-shattering events as I pursued God's highest calling on my life. I survived spiritual abuse at the hands of a controlling church leader. When I left, I lost every friend and every ministry position I had, and sat on a shelf for several years. During that time, I had no idea that God was moving me into my life's work, beginning with the launch of Awakening House of Prayer. Nor did I have a clue that He was going to make me the first-ever female editor of *Charisma* magazine. Some years later, my body started shutting down for no medical reason. I felt as if I were losing, day by day, everything I had built over the last twenty years. I was frustrated beyond measure. It was a spiritual attack. False prophets were cursing me, and it was affecting my health. When the curse was broken and I recovered, I walked away having learned to rest in spiritual warfare. It was a vital lesson for the next season. I had no idea that God would start sending me to the nations of the earth to raise up prophets to throw Jezebel off a wall (see 2 Kings 9:30–33).

You may not have to go through the extreme trials and tragedies I have endured—or maybe yours have been more intense. God does not bring those trials and tragedies, but He does use them to prepare us for our highest calling. Bishop Hamon's book will encourage you as you walk through your process. You will find understanding into why you are experiencing suffering, inspiration that keeps you from giving up and revelation that will put in you a determination to reach your highest calling in Christ. Every Christian needs to read this book.

Jennifer LeClaire, senior leader, Awakening House of Prayer
in Fort Lauderdale, Florida; founder, Ignite Network;
founder, Awakening Blaze prayer movement

Introduction

Out of the fourteen books that I have written, this one concerning God's highest calling is the most important. The truths found within this book will affect a Christian's eternal rewards and relationship with Jesus Christ throughout eternity. Understanding God's highest calling for His children gives wisdom and insight concerning the tests, trials and personal suffering that are experienced in life. Jesus declared that when we know the truth on a matter it sets us free to fulfill life without the horrible discouragement and frustrations that the average person experiences when facing difficult times.

In the first few chapters, we will discover some of the main reasons that motivated God to create man. Man had to be made a certain way from certain material and placed in a special place. This was necessary in order for God to fulfill His plans. We will see why man could not be made in heaven out of heavenly material. Man was completely new, different from all other created beings.

Man was a revelation to all, but the making of woman was a revolution. Angels had never seen such a beautiful and challenging creature in all their existence, for they do not have females in their race. At least there is no record in the Bible of someone seeing and talking to an angel and thinking it was a woman. Nevertheless, God created mankind as male and female to reproduce and fill the earth with a race in God's image and likeness. In the tenth chapter of this book, we will discuss additional reasons God had for man and woman marrying and becoming one.

Most preachers and most laypeople know that being conformed to the image and likeness of Jesus is God's highest calling for His children. What is not as well-known, however, is the process that God uses to fulfill His predestined purpose for us.

This process involves two principles: the Law of Transformation and the Process for Conformity to the image and likeness of Christ. A number of years ago, while a professor in a Christian college, I taught students the eight reasons or purposes that answer the question, Why man?, and explain what God wanted to accomplish through this race. Later I discussed these principles in my book *Who Am I and Why Am I Here?* The number one purpose, of course, was for Adam and Eve to reproduce themselves until the earth was filled with a race of humankind in God's image and likeness. Adam and Eve failed by disobeying God in the Garden of Eden; they lost their likeness of God in character and nature but kept their reproducing ability. Jesus Christ came four thousand years later and started a new race by, first, purchasing man with His blood shed on the cross. He then sent the Holy Spirit, who enabled individuals to be born again and, thereby, to become new creations in Christ—thus starting the new race of mankind called the "Church race."

In this new Church race, individuals are not recognized by natural nationality or as Jew or Gentile but by the name of *Christian*. These are God's special people whom He has chosen to be conformed to the likeness of His Son. God has appointed Jesus to be the head of this new race both now and throughout eternity. Those from this race who submit to and go through God's process for conforming them to the likeness of Christ in every area of His being will be chosen to rule and reign with Jesus in fulfilling God's eternal purposes.

In this book, I will be explaining the revelation of God's highest calling for individual Christians. I will share many ministries that we have fulfilled, but at this point I want to share the fact that there are seven major anointings upon my life and Christian International Ministries. I want to emphasize the one that has been the greatest blessing to my wife and me over the years, the "family anointing." Our three children have served the Lord all the days of their lives. They are all parents now of our eleven grandchildren and grandparents of our eighteen great-grandchildren. All three are major leaders in Christian International Ministries. They all prophesy and preach, and we have all written books. In fact, my daughter, Sherilyn, has just finished her first book, *Stewarding Your Best Life*. It is complementary to this book as it talks about the fact that you own nothing, but you owe everything to Jesus Christ. Jesus bought us body, soul and spirit with His blood. Everything we are and have belongs to Jesus. We are the stewards and managers of all that God has given us. Our rewards will be based on how we manage all He has given to us.

Our key Scripture for this study will be Romans 8:28–29:

> And we know that all things work together for good to those who love God, to those who are the called according to His purpose. For whom He foreknew, He also predestined to be conformed to the image of His Son, that He might be the firstborn among many brethren.

In chapter after chapter, I will be using various Scriptures, biblical examples and personal experiences to show *how* all things do work together for good to those who love God and are called according to His purpose of having each one conformed to the likeness of His Son so that Jesus will be the firstborn among many who are in His likeness. When you understand the application of two illustrations we will be discussing—first, of the thumb and fingers representing the inner man and the outer man and, second, the law of aerodynamics versus the law of gravity—you will understand how God can put you through trials that seem to be against His general will and yet are in His higher will as part of your processing. It will knock the "why" out of the trials and tests you go through.

I have numerous testimonies from those who went through my Mentoring Day where these truths were taught and became birthed within them. This changed their lives, helping them to go forward more victoriously as Christians. You will experience the same by the time you have finished reading this book.

I am grateful that Jesus called and anointed me to be a pioneer in the restoration of His Church. I am seeking with all I am and have to fulfill all He has given me to do. I want to hear the words, "Well done, good and faithful servant!" But I am more thankful that He revealed to me what His highest calling is: to be conformed to His image and likeness, mature sons and daughters whom He can trust with His affairs and eternal Kingdom.

1

God's Purpose for His Greatest Creation

And the LORD God formed man of the dust of the ground, and breathed into his nostrils the breath of life; and man became a living being.

Genesis 2:7

To understand God's highest calling for humankind we must discover all the many reasons God had for creating the human race.

God was not alone when He created humankind; He did not create people because He was lonely. Fellowship is one reason for our existence, but there were other factors that were more meaningful and purposeful to God.

Before Man Came into Being

Heaven, in fact, was filled with several types of creatures that God had made in the eternal past before He made man. The

Bible reveals three types of heavenly spirit beings that were with Him in His domain before man appeared on the earth. There are trillions of angels, which we will call the angelic race. There are also numerous cherubim and seraphim. Each of these three groups of beings looks different from the others and has different functions to perform.

But somewhere in the eternal past God planned the whole eternal future, which included the creation of man. Sometime in the beginning, when there was no one and nothing but God, He conceived of the plan to create the heavens and the earth. In fact, everything that now fills endless space, including the far reaches of our universe, was planned by God. He created the cherubim, seraphim and angels, but He also had plans to create a new race of beings who would be different from anything He had created before.

At the Right Time, a New Race

When the time was right God activated His plan to create this new race that would fulfill many desires and purposes for Him. When we use the word *time*, we are expressing earthly terminology, because there was no such thing as years, months, days, hours—not until God established earth as the place where He would put His special and unique creation. He would call this new race of being *man*.

This book is written to that race to which you and I belong. We will answer such questions as, Why did God create the human race? We will discover why some of God's plans and purposes for us required that man not be made in heaven out of heavenly material but from the dust of the planet called earth. We will reveal several things God wanted to accomplish through humankind. We will discover why the human race is called to be the highest race in the universe. We will then concentrate on the highest calling for every member of the human race—especially those who have become members of the new race, the Church race. There is a reason why everything had to be exactly the way God established it.

Our Goal: To Understand the Process

If I asked you about the reason for the creation of humankind, you would most likely know that it is Father God's will for His people to be conformed into the image and likeness of Jesus Christ, His Son. Most Christians know this. What is not as well-known is the process God uses to fulfill that purpose.

I am establishing two terms in this book to represent how God accomplishes His purpose for His sons and daughters to be like Jesus. Both phrases will be capitalized as proper nouns to show their importance in representing the main subject of the book—the method God uses to conform redeemed ones into the likeness of Christ Jesus. These descriptive terms will be used many times throughout the book: the Law of Transformation and God's Process for Conformity, or simply Transformation and Process. Many biblical and personal stories will help illustrate these terms and make them real.

I rarely have time to preach this truth in the pulpit. That is one of the main reasons I started conducting a Mentoring Day, which imparts the truths found in this book. Most of my pulpit preaching throughout the world deals with the restoration movements within the Church—where the Church is right now in God's present and progressive purpose for her. I was privileged to be commissioned to pioneer the Prophetic movement that was birthed in 1988. We prophesied the Saints movement that was birthed in 2007. The Third Reformation in 2008 and the Army of the Lord movement activated offensive spiritual warfare in 2016. I wrote books on each one of these moves of God.

This book is different in that it deals with the individual as opposed to the corporate Church. Here you will discover truths that will enlighten and endow you with the wisdom and power to make your life and ministry victorious to the end.

Trials and Rewards in the Process

There is one further thing I want you to know. I will not be writing much about my successes and what I have accomplished in life, for this book is about God's process for conforming us to the image and likeness of Jesus Christ. But I will mention one or two of the glorious, life-fulfilling, joyous times my wife and I experienced. I do not want you to think that we lived through one continuous trial, for the tests came only when God saw that we were ready to go through the Process again to reach our next level. Since most of the truths that will be presented here come from the writings of the apostle Paul, I will take the attitude that Paul took. When Paul talks about his infirmities, he includes those things that made him weak in the natural and what natural things he lost by going through the conforming Process. This includes his tests, trials, suffering, persecution—everything in the natural that seemed to be a negative experience in his life. Paul wrote: "If I must boast, I will boast in the things which concern my infirmity. . . . I will not boast, except in my infirmities" (2 Corinthians 11:30; 12:5).

But along with the trials, like Paul, I want to mention a few of God's blessings that came to us in order to encourage you that God does promote and reward His children after every Process for Conformity that we allow Him to take us through. God's tests and trials during the Process are not continuous. Just as tests in school are given at the end of a learning session or at the end of the school year, to determine whether or not we are ready to graduate to the next level, so after every conforming Process, God gives a greater ministry and rewards us in many ways. The harder He allowed me to be thrown down, the higher Jesus enabled me to bounce back—like a super-bounce rubber ball!

Here is one example of reward and favor for letting God take me through the Process for Conformity into the likeness of His Son. Between 1969 and 1972, I was going through the Process: There were two betrayals, my preaching ministry was greatly reduced and there were some heartbreaking and hopeless situations.

Yet at the end of that Process, on January 24, 1973, God gave me a divine visitation that enabled me to prophesy to numerous people for several continuous hours. He also gave me the revelation and ability to activate and train others in prophetic ministry. God gave me the anointing to be a reproducer of reproducers who would reproduce other reproducers of prophets and prophetic ministry. This resulted in my prophesying over the following forty years to more than fifty thousand individuals, from babies to kings and presidents of nations, and training more than five hundred thousand people in prophetic ministry in every continent of the world. I was honored to be named by *Charisma* magazine, in an issue dedicated to ministers who have most influenced the Church in the past four decades, as the pioneering father of the Prophetic movement. This came after 64 years of ministry and many, many Processes for Conformity to the likeness of Jesus Christ.

Your Own Journey Begins

As you read this book, you might think, *Could all that he and his wife went through have been purposed by God? Was it worth it all?* I can say, yes, absolutely, during this life and more so in the life to come throughout eternity. By the time you have finished reading this book, you will be able to say the same with great conviction and confidence.

You are embarking on an enlightening and challenging journey that will bring revelation and transformation into your life and enable you to fulfill God's highest calling for you. I believe that we all desire to become the kind of persons that God wants with Him throughout eternity. We want to hear those very important words from our Creator: "Well done, good and faithful servant! You fulfilled My highest calling for you. You fulfilled the membership ministry I gave you when I baptized you into the Body of Christ. Come now and live and reign with Me throughout eternity."

ACKNOWLEDGMENT & PETITION

Almighty God, I acknowledge that You created humankind. Your first couple failed, but You sent Your Son, and He fulfilled and demonstrated the type of person You want. I want to be Your type of person, like Jesus. I surrender my all to Your Process to grow me in Christlikeness.

2

What Is Man?

"What is man that You are mindful of him, or the son of man that You take care of him?"

Hebrews 2:6

The Bible makes it clear that God created humans with His own two hands and breathed into them an eternal spirit. Animals have lungs and breathe air as well, but God did not breathe His breath of life into them as He did with man. That is the reason humankind has an eternal spirit and the capacity to be resurrected bodily but animals do not. Humans did not evolve from a lower species, developing gradually. God created Adam and Eve not as babies but as full-grown intelligent individuals. Those who propagate the theory of evolution are basing it on human imagination without factual scientific proof. This is mainly because natural man does not want to acknowledge that there is a God who created everything—including humankind.

The Biblical Record of Man on Planet Earth

The plans and purposes God had for creating this special race required that humankind be made a certain way and be placed in a specific area. God could not place man in heaven, for He knew that man would end up sinning. Sin cannot be allowed in heaven, nor could man continue living in sin in heaven. Man had to exist and function outside of God's throne area. His home had to be outside of heaven on a planet in a certain part of the universe.

God chose a distant planet in one of the solar systems within the Milky Way galaxy. Planet earth is located some 27,000 light-years from the center of this galaxy. (A light-year is how far light travels at 186,287 miles per second in one year, which is about six trillion miles. Our Milky Way galaxy is 200,000 light-years across.) It is just one of multi-millions of galaxies in God's universe. If humankind could develop the ability to travel at the speed of light, it would still take 200,000 years to travel across our galaxy. We don't know whether heaven's throne is light-years away or in a different dimension.

Earth was to be man's home for an indefinite period. The body of man was made from the dust of the earth, to live on the earth and to have dominion over everything on the earth.

> Then God said, "Let Us make man in Our image, according to Our likeness; let them have dominion over the fish of the sea, over the birds of the air, and over the cattle, over all the earth and over every creeping thing that creeps on the earth." So God created man in His own image; in the image of God He created him; male and female He created them. Then God blessed them, and God said to them, "Be fruitful

and multiply; fill the earth and subdue it; have dominion over the fish of the sea, over the birds of the air, and over every living thing that moves on the earth."

Genesis 1:26–28

And the LORD God formed man of the dust of the ground, and breathed into his nostrils the breath of life; and man became a living being.

Genesis 2:7

God made a special place on the earth where the humans would live (see Genesis 2:8). He brought from heaven seeds from the trees, flowers, fruit trees and the rest of the vegetation and planted them in a special area and named that great park the Garden of Eden. That gave man a little piece of heaven on earth. Jesus has made a place of heaven on earth for us to live in called *a heavenly place in Christ Jesus*: "[God] made us alive together with Christ . . . and made us sit together in the heavenly places in Christ Jesus" (Ephesians 2:5–6).

The Physical Body of Man

This special creature called *man* had to be made a certain way in order to fulfill all the purposes for which God was creating him. Man was made different from the angels. God had so many things planned for man to fulfill that nothing less than being made in God's own image and likeness would do. *Image* means to look like God's bodily appearance. *Likeness* means to have Godlike attributes, character and capabilities. Man was made with an independent life, in that God gave him the power and right to make decisions on his own. Man could say yes or no to God's commands and will. He could also say yes or no to any of the devil's suggestions. He had the power of choice. Adam was, therefore, a free moral agent.

When God was designing the human body, He not only had Himself as a pattern but also was thinking of the body that He wanted His Son to have when He came to earth to be a man. Jesus would have that body while He walked the earth as a mortal; it would be crucified and placed in a grave. But Father God would resurrect that mankind body to be an immortal and eternal flesh-and-bone body. Jesus is now sitting at the right hand of God in that body. Jesus, God the Son, will live and reign in that body forever. When He returns, all the saints will have their bodies translated or resurrected to be like His resurrected, glorious mankind body (see 1 Thessalonians 5:23).

God's Commission to Adam

God put Adam in the paradisiacal Garden and gave two commissions to him. The first was to reproduce himself, and the second was to take dominion over everything God had put on the earth. God told him to go to work by taking care of it, by keeping it in good shape, which was physical work. He then told him to do some mental work by naming all the birds of the air and animals of the field.

I can imagine Adam asking, "What names do I give all the creatures You created?"

And God responding, "Whatever name you give them will be fine. I want you to exercise your will and name them whatever you want. My will is for you to name them with the creative mind I gave you. I created this earth and fixed it up for you. It is yours to rule and enjoy with the wisdom I put within you. Remember, I am the one who created you to look like Me outwardly and have the inner motivation of My heart and the thoughts of My mind. I gave all this for your joy and fulfillment. I am your Creator-Father, and you have inherited much of My DNA (divine nature attributes) and abilities."

God would likely continue, "It is My pleasure to give you the kingdom of this world to be your home and the place where you will raise your family. I am appointing you to take care of and develop this earth the same as I would. I am not going to do it for you. I have put within you all you need to govern this earth. I will be visiting with you and will be available to help if you encounter something you do not know how to handle. But I am not going to be holding your hand all the time and telling you everything to do. Use your heart, mind and hands that I gave you. I will be watching over you from heaven 24 hours a day. When you face something that is bigger than you and seemingly beyond your present capabilities, just call upon Me and I will be a present help in your time of need" (see Hebrews 4:16).

Adam's Need That He Could Not Meet

So Adam started naming all the creatures, and he began noticing something that seemed to be consistent. There would be two animals that looked alike, but each member of the pair was different from the other. One had male characteristics like him, but the other had different characteristics. Since God had named him *man*, he would call the one that looked more like him *male* and the other one *female*. He noticed they were comparable and compatible with each other. When he named the long-necked creature *giraffe* there was a male and female. The same was true with the horse, dog, cow, monkey, lion and ape. He kept looking for someone who would be comparable and compatible with him.

God came by one day and noticed that Adam looked a little sad and confused.

Adam said, "Lord, I have noticed something. You told me to use my mind and think things through. I have noticed that every male animal has a female that looks like him and seems to be comparable and compatible. I am a male, but I have not found my female that is like me, somehow different but comparable and compatible."

God said to Adam, "Didn't I tell you that if you found a need you couldn't meet, I would do for you what you couldn't do for yourself? Come and lie down here and let me give you a knockout drop, and when you wake up, I think you will love what I will have for you."

God opened Adam's side, took out a rib and closed the flesh back up. God took that rib and made a woman.

Adam awoke, opened his eyes and saw her. He jumped up with great excitement and said, "You shall be my wife and co-reign with me over all things on earth. I will call you Eve, for you shall be the mother of all living. You shall now be bone of my bone and flesh of my flesh for you were taken from my side" (see Ephesians 5:30–32).

God did not make Eve from the dust of the earth as He did Adam but made her from substance taken from Adam's side. This becomes symbolic of the Bride of Christ being taken from the pierced side of Jesus Christ.

After my wife and I were married, I would tease her by saying, "You know, the first woe to man was 'woe-man'—woman." Then I would say, "God made man first, then after that He made woman, and woman has been after man ever since!"

One day she got back at me.

She said, "Honey, I read in the Bible that man was made out of just common dirt, but woman was not made out of dirt. Woman was made out of refined flesh—and woman has been that far advanced beyond man ever since!"

The Garden: A Little Bit of Heaven

Adam and Eve lived in Eden for an unknown amount of time. But they were not allowed to stay indefinitely. The reason for this had to do with the two unique trees God had put right in the middle of the Garden. They could eat of the Tree of Life, which would allow them to keep living as long as they kept eating of it. But God had put another tree there that He commanded them not to eat of, for if they did death would begin to work in their bodies, and they would die.

One day Eve became curious about the Tree of Knowledge of Good and Evil.

Satan had come to her in the form of the serpent and had said, "Have you noticed how pleasant the fruit on this tree looks to your eyes? It has a tantalizing taste—greater than that of any other fruit you have eaten in the Garden. If you will eat of it, you will become very wise like God Himself."

Eve ate of the fruit of the tree and gave some to Adam, and he ate also. When they did, something happened to them. They saw things with their eyes that they had not knowingly seen before. They looked at each other and realized they had been walking with God all this time naked.

New strange feelings flooded their souls—self-consciousness, fear, shame. Suddenly they felt a desire to hide from God instead of joining Him joyfully for their times of fellowship together. When God came to spend time with Adam and Eve, they were not where they were supposed to be.

God called out to Adam, "Where are you?"

Adam answered fearfully, "When we heard You coming we hid and have covered our nakedness with fig leaves."

God asked, "Did you eat of the forbidden fruit that I commanded you not to eat of?"

They had to admit they had.

God's Judgment on Man's Disobedience

God pronounced judgment upon the man and woman and upon the serpent who had tricked Eve into eating the fruit. God had to cast the man and woman out of the Garden lest they eat of the Tree of Life in their sinful state. This was the beginning of sin in the human race—which brought the sickness, sorrow and death that continue to the present day. They lost their innocence and purity, which started a chain reaction of sin and corruption ending in death to themselves and all future generations of humankind. Humans continued to degenerate and corrupt themselves until some 1,600 years later when God looked at the human race and saw that it was corrupt to the core.

Mankind's every thought was now motivated by lust of the flesh, lust of the eyes and pride of life (see Genesis 6:11–13; 1 John 2:16). God was greatly disappointed that they had become the very opposite of the way He had made them. God wanted them to be like Him. They had become more like Lucifer, the archangel who rebelled against God and was cast out of heaven. He became known as Satan, the devil and a few other names (see Revelation 12:9). Satan degenerated into the very personification of all evil, and his angels into wicked, demonic creatures.

In the ages before the creation of humankind, when Lucifer was cast out of heaven and down to earth, it caused a cataclysmic explosion that destroyed all of the vegetation. Earth became flooded with water and frozen into one big ice ball in gross darkness. This became Satan's prison. The earth was in that state for an indefinite period of time until God came and fixed it back up for man's habitation. This is the reason Genesis 1:2 describes the earth as being without form and void of light, a desolate wasteland. I imagine the archangels Gabriel and Michael wondering why God had chosen this place of Satan's prison as the home for His new human creation.

Preparing Earth for Habitation

God is light, so when the Creator spoke His will regarding the earth, it lit up with divine cosmic light. God took six days to restore the earth and the atmosphere around it. By the third day the frozen waters around the earth had melted, so God separated the land, raising it above the water, which began to flow and form oceans, seas, lakes and rivers. Then God created birds to fly in the air, fish to swim in the waters and animals to cover the land. On the last half of the sixth day God made man from the dust of the earth. This began the era of humankind on planet earth (see Genesis 1:1–2:7).

But humans, as we have seen, did not choose to remain in this perfection. If we count the years in the genealogy given in Genesis 5 and Genesis 7:6, we can compute that 1,656 years after the Fall, humankind had degenerated and corrupted itself to be more like Lucifer and his fallen angels than like the human being God had created in His own image and likeness. Humankind had become worthless to God, so He decided to remove those humans from the earth and send their spirit beings to the devil's hellish kingdom of darkness.

Why Noah and an Ark?

Almighty God directed Noah to build an Ark and take aboard with him his family, a pair of every kind of animal and seven pairs each of the clean animals and birds (see Genesis 7:2–3). God had decided that He was going to wipe the wicked people—estimated at some twenty million—off the face of the earth with a great flood, but preserve and reestablish the human race and the animal kingdom. The floodwaters covered the highest mountain by more than twenty feet, which left neither man nor animal alive on earth except the eight humans in the Ark and the creatures preserved there.

Some have wondered why God did not just blast the earth into cosmic dust with everything living on it, since this model of humankind seemed to be faulty and not worthy of continuing. It could also be argued that God had seemed to place humans in the wrong spot, because Satan was there to corrupt them. Why not just choose another planet, make another couple and start all over again? Maybe the new model of humankind He made this time would work perfectly. If Noah was the only righteous man on earth and God wanted to save him, then God could have translated him to heaven as He did Enoch (see Genesis 5:24; Hebrews 11:5).

The story gives the appearance that God's humankind project had failed. Yet that is not the case. God's overall eternal plan with the purpose He wanted to accomplish was right on schedule. We will discover in this book how God will still fulfill the eight major reasons for which He created the human race on earth.

We will reveal how it can look as if your plans and projects have failed, how it appears that all has been lost and how you regret the mistakes you have made. But just as God looked at this desperate situation on the earth and made it successful in the end, so He will do for you in your most difficult trials. God did it for Job, and He can do it for you (see Job 42:10).

God Declares Bankruptcy

I was speaking to some Christian businessmen after the 2008 stock market crash. Some of those men had to declare their businesses bankrupt. They were feeling ashamed and embarrassed, for they felt Christians should not declare bankruptcy. Bankruptcy happens when one's liabilities are so much greater than one's assets that there is just no other way to survive the situation. It allows individuals to liquidate their liabilities, take what little assets are left and start over somewhere else.

That is what happened to God's "humankind business." He had millions of human liabilities and only eight assets.

He declared bankruptcy, liquidated His liabilities, took His few assets, transferred them to another place and started all over again. Corrupted humankind was an enormous liability; Noah and his family were His few assets. God understands humankind and all the problems we have, but He uses those things to transform and conform His people. We will reveal how all these things work together for good to bring us to our destiny of being conformed to the likeness of Christ Jesus.

ACKNOWLEDGMENT & PETITION

Lord, You knew that humans would eventually sin and become subject to death. Yet You seemed to be surprised that humankind degenerated so far from what You created us to be. Your heart was grieved. You had to destroy them all. But You directed Noah to build an Ark to preserve and continue the human race. You had a master plan beyond the comprehension of mortal man. You have revealed much to us these days. Father, help us know Your full plan. Reveal it to Your people so that we can co-labor with You in finalizing Your purpose for mortal man and Your Church.

3

God's Highest Desire and Purpose in Creating Man

Then God said, "Let Us make man in Our image, according to Our likeness. . . ." So God created man in His own image; in the image of God He created him; male and female He created them. . . . And man became a living being.

Genesis 1:26–27; 2:7

Before God created man and breathed an eternal spirit into him, He planned man's creation to the minute detail. He planned for man to be mortal; in order to maintain life, Adam and Eve had to eat continually from the Tree of Life. The moment they ate of the Tree of Knowledge of Good and Evil, death began to work in their bodies. God removed their access to the Tree of Life, and 930 years later Adam's body died. It was necessary for man to be mortal in order for Jesus to take on a mortal body and die in man's place.

God knew that man would sin and need a means of redemption; nevertheless, God planned for humans to co-labor with Him eternally. Thus, when man's body died, his spirit would continue to exist and function in the spiritual dimension. The righteous would live in God's heavenly realms, and the unrighteous would live in the place called hell that God had prepared for the devil and his fallen angels (see Matthew 25:46).

The Kind of Human Creature God Wanted

God wanted a being in His image and likeness that was sovereign—meaning that man would have the free will to decide for himself what choices he would make and what actions he would take. God knew when He designed this free moral agent that man could rebel against Him and live his own life. But God did not want slaves or mechanical robots. Father God wanted true sons and daughters who were born of God having and manifesting His own DNA. He wanted living body, soul and spirit human beings. He did not want His people to serve Him and relate to Him out of force or out of fear of the consequences if they did not live the way God intended them to live.

God wanted man to know Him, to understand who He is, to love Him, to believe that He is a good, holy, righteous and true God. Almighty God wanted man by free choice to relate willingly to his Creator, to be convinced that God's way of living and His standards of right and wrong are best. He wanted man to be confident that God's way is the only right way—the only way to be, the only truth to believe, the only life to live. Sad to say, this is not the condition of most Christians today. Very few believers have matured to the state of thinking and being like Jesus.

Awakened by a False Challenge

There was a time in my Christian life when God illuminated my thinking concerning His desire and purpose for humankind. In my second year of pastoring, when I was 21 years old, I visited a church within our church's area of fellowship as I was curious to hear their guest speaker.

The minister indicated that he was offering a new revelation about God and His plans for humankind. His revelation was nothing but a repeat of a false doctrine that has been preached within the Church since the 1600s during the Protestant movement. It was the doctrine of the restoration of all things, including the devil, all of his fallen angels and every human being who has ever lived on planet earth.

The preacher took certain Scriptures and misapplied their meanings in such a way as to make the false doctrine sound like truth. He paraphrased verses such as, "It is not God's will that any should perish." He used a verse from the apostle Paul to explain that physical death came upon the whole human race because of Adam's sin, but that everyone would be resurrected bodily because of Jesus Christ. He twisted that Scripture to say that, as in Adam all were made sinners, in Christ all were made sanctified enough to be allowed into heaven.

He went on to ask that since God is love, can anyone imagine a loving Father taking man that He made in His own image and fallen angels that He created and casting them into a burning hell to be tormented forever? He emphasized that *all* would be redeemed: sinful mankind, fallen angels and Satan himself would be in heaven. He proclaimed emphatically that his teaching was magnifying Jesus as our wonderful Savior, full of love, grace and forgiveness.

He gave his challenge with a pleading voice: "Doesn't that make you want to serve such a loving and merciful God?"

Some of the more immature believers were responding with tears in their eyes, saying, "Oh, isn't God loving and forgiving? He is going to restore everyone and everything to be one united and happy family with Jesus in heaven forever!"

The church members did not realize that he was teaching a false doctrine called Universalism. It sounds wonderful and humanistic and supposedly greatly magnifies the love and grace of God, but the fact is that the Bible stresses emphatically that heaven and hell are two separate places that will never be united throughout eternity. Once a person dies there is no opportunity to change his or her destiny. Only those who believe in Jesus Christ and whose names are written in the Lamb's Book of Life will be in heaven. All others will spend eternity in the hellish lake of fire. Revelation 20:15 is clear on this point: "Anyone not found written in the Book of Life was cast into the lake of fire."

The Holy Spirit Steps In

As I drove home that night, I was very upset and frustrated by all that I had heard. I was alone in the car and began to reason with myself. If the devil, his fallen angels and all wicked humanity are going to get into heaven, the same as me—a person with a born-again experience, living a life of self-denial and not participating in any forbidden pleasures of the world—then what profit is there in my living the Christian way of life? If all of them are going to receive all the benefits of heaven, the same as believers, then what is the advantage of denying oneself and sacrificing for the cause of Christ?

I made the following statement out loud as I deliberated the matter: "I might as well go out and live and do as I please, if what that preacher preached is the truth."

When I said that, the Holy Spirit asked me a question. *Bill Hamon, are you saying that if it were not for your fear of hell or the hope of going to heaven, you would not live the Christian life?*

I knew that when God asks you a question, He is doing it to get you to think and analyze. I knew also that He was not implying that there is not an eternal hell and heaven, but rather He wanted me to think about what my statement implied.

He then asked me another question: *If I should decree that all the world and humankind are now eternal, and everything is to continue to function as it is, would you still think that God's way of living is the best way for you and the whole human race to live?*

It made me contemplate the situation anew. If there were not a hell to avoid or a heaven to gain would I still live the life of Christ? In other words, was I doing what God's Word said was right and not doing what it said was wrong only to escape hell and gain heaven? If so, then I was outwardly conforming to what God's Word declares is the only route to heaven, but inwardly I was not convinced that God's way of life was the best way for me to live my mortal life on earth.

He likened me to the very religious Pharisees who conformed outwardly to God's commands but inwardly were doing it only to avoid God's judgment. The Holy Spirit reminded me of what Jesus said to His followers: "Unless your righteousness exceeds the righteousness of the scribes and Pharisees, you will by no means enter the kingdom of heaven" (Matthew 5:20).

Birthing of the Revelation

That is when I began to receive the revelation and conviction that God's highest calling and purpose for each one of His children is to be conformed to the image of His Son, Christ Jesus. My success on earth and reward in heaven would not be based on how great a pastor, prophet or evangelist I became here on earth but rather on how much I became conformed to the life of Christ in His thinking, attitude and actions.

If I was to have the privilege of ruling and reigning as a joint heir with Christ, then I had to be transformed into God's way of thinking, His attitude and convictions. I had to be convinced that God is just, right and holy in all His ways. If I was not convinced in this life, could Jesus trust me with His affairs in the world to come? Could Father God trust me as much as He trusted His only begotten Son to follow through and do everything exactly the way God wanted me to do it?

To be conformed to the likeness of Jesus Christ is to have His selflessness and to move in faithful obedience, unwavering dedication and complete trust in God. It means that even when He asks you to accomplish something for Him—and you count the mental, emotional and physical cost, something that sounds so horrible you cringe in agony—you answer Him by saying, "If there is no other way for Your will to be accomplished, Father, then I submit. Not my will but Yours be done." His only begotten Son prayed that way in the Garden of Gethsemane. The apostle Paul prayed that way as well.

> I also count all things loss for the excellence of the knowledge of Christ Jesus my Lord, for whom I have suffered the loss of all things, and count them as rubbish, that I may gain Christ . . . that I may know Him and the power of His resurrection, and the fellowship of His sufferings, being conformed to His death.
>
> Philippians 3:8, 10

Abraham was told by God to do a horrible, heartbreaking thing, but Abraham submitted immediately to God's will even though it sounded illogical and unreasonable. God told him to take his only son, Isaac, whom he dearly loved, and offer him as a sacrifice. It not only challenged Abraham's heart as a father, but it seemed to put into jeopardy all the promises that God had said would be fulfilled through this son. No wonder Abraham is called the father of the faithful believers (see Romans 4:16–22).

Later in this book when we explore God's Process for Conformity and the Law of Transformation, I will give more personal and biblical illustrations of what we have to go through during this life to reach conformity to the likeness of Jesus.

The Power to Think and Live Independently

We have established that God wanted a being in His image and likeness who was a free moral agent. To have the type of person God wanted, He could not make the living being preprogrammed so that he could think only God's thoughts. He needed to make him pure and innocent with free will and the potential to think not only God's thoughts but also his own thoughts and even those Satan would suggest to him.

After man ate of the Tree of Knowledge of Good and Evil, he knew there was right and wrong, good and evil, a bad devil and a good God. Even after man sinned, he still had God's creative ability through his imagination to create his own thoughts. Every thought of man is not always from God or the devil. Man can create his own thoughts. When man was put outside the Garden, he had to learn to choose the Creator as His God and Savior and learn the Lord's way of right living.

Adam and Eve also retained the ability to procreate more individuals with the ability to think independently. When God created Adam and Eve, He told them that He had given them the power through procreation to reproduce other human beings like themselves. God would not be creating any more human beings, for He had created Adam and Eve to be the father and mother of the rest of the human race. The rest of the people to live on the earth would have to be born into this world. God then commissioned them to procreate and multiply the human race until they inhabited the whole earth.

God gave this command to Adam and Eve in the Garden before they sinned. If man had never sinned, God's plan for humankind was for them to fill the earth with a race of humankind in their own image—which was in the image and likeness of God. Adam and Eve sinned and failed to fulfill that plan. But four thousand years later Jesus would come and start a new race of humankind to fill the earth with people who had matured into God's own image and likeness. (See 1 Corinthians 12:27; 2 Corinthians 5:17; Ephesians 2:14–16; 1 Peter 2:9–10.)

The Called-Out Church Race

Did God know all of this ahead of time? Yes, God knew when He made man a free moral agent that every human being would not relate to Him and be the type of humankind creation He wanted him or her to be. But God also knew He would not need every human that was born on earth to fulfill His purpose for creating man. His purpose was to accumulate a certain number who would believe in Him and be conformed to His image and likeness. (Remember: If one believes that the God of love should allow all humankind to be in heaven simply because He created them—in other words, because they never asked to be created—then that one would also have to agree to and endorse the false doctrine of Universalism. It would be like a 25-year-old son telling his parents that they have to support him and allow him to stay in their house, regardless of how he lives, because he never asked to be born to them.)

God's long-range plan was to send His only begotten Son, Jesus Christ, to shed His life's blood to redeem a people who would be a new creation of humankind. They would be a special race called out from the fallen human race—both

Jew and Gentile—and would be known in heaven and earth as the Church race. They would be a body of believers also known as the Body of Christ. The apostle Paul compared the Body of Christ to the human body, which is one body but with many members. It requires millions of members, from the mighty muscles to the microscopic molecules, to make a functioning human body (see 1 Corinthians 12:12–27).

Likewise, the same is true concerning the spiritual Body of Christ. The Body of Christ is a real living and functioning Body of true believers in Christ Jesus who have eternal life. Jesus is the Head of this Body, which is called, designed and designated to function forever. Jesus Christ needs a certain number of members to make His corporate Body complete. He needs prepared members to fulfill certain positions and functions. He also needs a certain number of overcomer saints who have been transformed to be like Him in all areas of their lives and who have qualified to rule and reign with Him.

Father God is perfecting those who are to co-labor with Christ in fulfilling His eternal purpose for cresting the human race. The mortal human race will continue living on earth until Jesus has sufficient qualified members to make His corporate Body complete. When that is accomplished, Jesus will come back to earth and remove all who are not members of His Body from the earth and restore the earth and its atmosphere with His cleansing fire. Then our old earth will become a new earth where only righteousness dwells. The apostle Peter declared that "we, according to His promise, look for new heavens and a new earth in which righteousness dwells" (2 Peter 3:13).

Thus we come to understand God's highest priority and greatest purpose for humankind: It is to be conformed to the nature and character of Jesus Christ in all areas. It is to become fully the likeness of Jesus Christ. Jesus was the model of God's perfect man and man's perfect God.

Foundations in Ministry

This book is going to cover truths that I rarely take the time to preach from the pulpit. I normally preach and demonstrate the restoration movements of the Church. In the 1980s and 1990s, I was preaching and writing books to help establish the Church in the truths and ministries of the Prophetic movement. I wrote three books and a large manual for teaching, activating and training the Church in prophetic ministry. At Christian International Ministries (CI) we conducted seminars and the School of the Holy Spirit to teach and train the saints to hear the voice of God and prophesy the word of the Lord to others.

In 1984 a major prophet prophesied that God had given me a special anointing to be a reproducer of reproducers who could do all that I was doing in the prophetic. This anointing has enabled us to train close to half a million believers in every continent in the world and most of the nations, even in China and Russia. We did the same with the Apostolic movement in the 1990s and the Saints movement in 2007. When the Third Reformation was decreed from heaven in 2008, I wrote the book that covered the first, second and third reformations called *Prophetic Scriptures Yet to Be Fulfilled*.

When the Army of the Lord movement was activated in 2016, I wrote the book describing what it is all about, called *God's Weapons of War*. For the last several years I have taught the truths in that book and led the Church in corporate spiritual warfare in thirty nations and hundreds of churches in the Americas.

You can see that I have had little time to preach on God's highest calling! Now this book will cover this truth that brings the Law of Transformation to God's people. This is the main truth I teach in my Mentoring Day courses. Some of my board of governors felt I should start having people come to me more instead of my continuing to travel more than two hundred thousand miles a year to the nations, especially since I am in my mideighties now. People come from Asia, Europe, Africa and the Virgin Islands.

Family Leaders and Board of Governors

I have a board of governors who work directly with me. They are dedicated to co-labor together to fulfill the vision and commission that God has given me. They pray for me and support our ministry financially. Most all of them head their own ministries or businesses. My board of governors consists of about thirty people. Several of them have been with me for more than thirty years.

Technically, three of them have been with me for most of my ministry life. Dr. Tim Hamon, my oldest son at age 63, is CEO of all Christian International organizations. Apostle Tom Hamon and his apostolic wife, Jane, have been with CI since their marriage in 1981. My daughter, Sherilyn, moved with her four children to Santa Rosa Beach, Florida, to be a part of CI in 2006. Sherilyn and her husband were one of the four couples that were part of the origination of the board of governors in 1985. Sherilyn is now administrative manager of the CI office staff and the administrator of my personal affairs and traveling ministry. These three are the bishopric executive team that will lead this ministry after I am gone. It is important to have a succession plan in place before the founder/vision-holder leaves the ministry.

Apostle Leon Walters has been with me since 1979 and has proven to be the best anyone could hope for in being a co-laborer with me. Leon is not only my brother-in-law but has proven to be a trustworthy and dedicated friend to me, my family and the CI ministry. His reward will be great. He has helped grow the ministry tremendously. Leon took over CI Central about 25 years ago and has built it to be the largest of the twelve CI regions.

My Vision Challenged to Increase and Expand

During the first fifty years of ministry, my vision and passion were to see all five ascension gift ministries restored back into the Church. The teacher, pastor and evangelist were recognized and accepted in the Church, but the prophet and apostle were not. My passion was to see all five fully functioning to fulfill their commission of equipping the saints in their membership ministries and manifesting the gifts of the Holy Spirit.

The apostle Paul presents this fully in Ephesians 4:11–15 and 1 Corinthians 12:7–11. Thank God that after thirty years of teaching, writing and training, I see that the apostle and prophet are recognized, accepted and functioning throughout the world! It is absolutely essential that the five-fold ministry and the gifts of the Holy Spirit be activated in order for Jesus to fulfill His end time purposes through the Church.

The Third and Final Church Reformation

In 2008 God revealed to me that the Third and final Church Reformation had been decreed from heaven to be activated on earth. I had to expand my vision and move my goal line from Ephesians 4:11–16 to Revelation 11:15. He told me:

> "Enlarge the place of your tent, and let them stretch out the curtains of your dwellings; do not spare; lengthen your cords, and strengthen your stakes. For you shall expand to the right and to the left, and your descendants will inherit the nations, and make the desolate cities inhabited.
>
> "Do not fear, for you will not be ashamed; neither be disgraced, for you will not be put to shame. . . . For your Maker is your husband, the LORD of hosts is His name; and your Redeemer is the Holy One of Israel; He is called the God of the whole earth."
>
> Isaiah 54:2–5

I had thought the final product that would bring about the Second Coming of Christ was a perfected, glorious Church ready to be presented to Jesus as His Bride. The Third Reformation does have that happening at the end of its ministry, but there are several things the matured Church must accomplish before the Church is made immortal. The Army of the Lord movement was activated in 2016 into the victorious, aggressive Church going on the offensive to fulfill the prophecies of Daniel 2:35, 44–45; 7:12–13, 18, 22, 26–27; and Revelation 11:15. Remember that Jesus will fulfill all end time prophecies in and through His corporate Body, the Church. Jesus will not return to earth in His personal body until He comes to resurrect and translate His saints and lead the saints army and angelic army in the final war where the devil and his army of fallen angels and the armies of wicked men are destroyed from the earth (see Revelation 19:11–21; 20:5–6). I have gone to thirty nations, teaching them how to do corporate warfare and training the saints for the consummation of the ages, which the final war will bring about.

Fulfilling Our Individual Highest Calling

Now Jesus is having me add the ministry of teaching and activating the saints into God's highest calling so that we can make it through all we must go through and do all we must do to fulfill God's final will for His mortal Church.

The restoration and activation of the fivefold ministry, the gifts of the Spirit activated and functioning in the saints and the revelation and activation of God's great army—all of these are essential for fulfilling God's work He has predestined for the Third Reformation Church to do. Nevertheless, it is not God's highest calling for His individual children. God has a personal and intimate purpose for His special ones.

The personal goal and dominant desire of every child of God should be conformity to the likeness of Jesus. I have discovered through my 66 years of ministry that if any saint—including any preacher—has any other ambitious goal above this one, then he or she is being set up for many disappointing, confusing and discouraging times. I have seen several church members and ministers fall away from serving the Lord because they did not understand God's process for fulfilling His highest purpose in their lives. By the time we cover the major processes God uses to perfect us in Christ

Jesus, it will knock the "why" out of your thinking *Why me, Lord? Why did this happen?* There will be no more "why this" and "why that" in your conversation because you will understand why. You will have grasped the biblical understanding of the challenging and traumatic things that happen in the lives of believers.

Jesus Experienced the Human Life

Here are abbreviated definitions of the Law of Transformation and the Process for Conformity:

> The *Law of Transformation* means decentralizing man from his carnal, natural, selfish self-life.
> The *Process for Conformity* means conforming that self-life to the life of Christ.

Read the Scriptures below in both translations and take note of some special statements that proclaim the truths of the Law of Transformation and the Process for Conformity. If Jesus had to learn obedience by the things He suffered, and if He qualified to be the Captain of our salvation through tests, trials and suffering, you can imagine that we will need to go through some of the same to be conformed to His likeness.

> For it was fitting for Him, for whom are all things and by whom are all things, in bringing many sons to glory [Christlikeness], to make the captain of their salvation perfect through sufferings. . . . Inasmuch then as the children have partaken of flesh and blood, He Himself likewise shared in

the same, that through death He might destroy him who had the power of death, that is, the devil, and release those who through fear of death were all their lifetime subject to bondage. For indeed [Jesus] does not give aid to angels, but He does give aid to the seed of Abraham. Therefore, in all things [Jesus] had to be made like His brethren, that He might be a merciful and faithful High Priest in things pertaining to God, to make propitiation for the sins of the people. For in that He Himself has suffered, being tempted, He is able to aid those who are tempted.

Hebrews 2:10, 14–18

It makes good sense that the God who got everything started and keeps everything going now completes the work by making the Salvation Pioneer perfect through suffering as he leads all these people to glory. Since the One who saves and those who are saved have a common origin, Jesus doesn't hesitate to treat them as family, saying,

I'll tell my good friends, my brothers and sisters, all I know about you [Father]; I'll join them in worship and praise to you.

Again, [Jesus] puts himself in the same family circle when he says,

Even I live by placing my trust in God.

And yet again,

I'm here with the children God gave me.

Since the children are made of flesh and blood, it's logical that the Savior took on flesh and blood in order to rescue them by his death. By embracing death, taking it into himself, he destroyed the Devil's hold on death and freed all who cower through life, scared to death of death.

It's obvious, of course, that he didn't go to all this trouble for angels. It was for people like us, children of Abraham. That's why he had to enter into every detail of human life. Then, when he came before God as high priest to get rid of the people's sins, he would have already experienced it all himself—all the pain, all the testing—and would be able to help where help was needed.

Hebrews 2:10–18 MESSAGE

Jesus "had to enter into every detail of human life." Yes, Jesus knows what life is like for humankind on earth.

Requirements to Head This New Race

The Bible says, "There is one God and one Mediator between God and men, that is, the Man Christ Jesus" (1 Timothy 2:5). Jesus, through His life, death and resurrection, became qualified to be the head of the redeemed human race. Father God had Jesus come to earth as a mortal and live as one among them. His first thirty years on earth gave Him the opportunity to grow up in all the stages that we go through from childhood to adulthood. He can understand our lives regardless of what stage of life we are in. That is one reason why Jesus referred to Himself as the Son of man.

The Bible and history reveal that Joseph, who was the stepfather of Jesus, was a general contractor in masonry and carpentry building. Tradition tells us that Joseph died when Jesus was fifteen years old. That means Jesus, being the old-est in the family of four younger brothers and a number of sisters, had to take over as head of the household and had to take responsibility for running the business. No doubt Joseph had trained his oldest son in both the work and management of the business. Jewish custom expected the oldest son to go into business with his father and continue the business when the father died.

What responsibility for a fifteen-year-old! Usually men working in that trade are fairly rough and tough. Jesus learned many things about human nature by being the boss. No doubt his brothers worked with Him in the business as they grew older. Mark 6:3 gives us the names of His brothers. If we make the estimate that the siblings were born about two years apart, then when Jesus was fifteen, James would have been thirteen, Joses eleven, Judas nine and Simon seven. The verse just says "sisters," which means there were two or more. If we also surmise that Jesus' mother, Mary, was eighteen when she birthed Jesus, she would have been only 33 years old at this time.

Just think about it. God had Jesus spend thirty years being a man and only three and a half years being a minister. God placed ten times more importance on His manhood than His ministry. This is another proof that God's highest calling is not being the greatest *minister* but rather being the image and likeness of the *man* Christ Jesus. Be assured, Jesus knows the challenges of managing the family business and providing for a family of eight.

When Jesus was launched into His divine ministry at the age of thirty, He had to organize the business for his brothers to take over and carry on. Jesus was thrown into the limelight after being baptized in water, tempted by the devil after fasting forty days, anointed with the Holy Spirit and power and beginning His ministry as the manifest Son of God. He also had to choose twelve men to mentor who would then carry on His work after He was gone. (See Matthew 4:1–2; 10:1–5; Acts 10:38.)

Making Disciples into Apostles

Jesus had an inner circle of three among His specially chosen twelve disciples: brothers James and John, and Peter. Peter's brother, Andrew, was the one who brought Peter to Jesus, but he was not in the inner-circle group. Before Jesus finished His ministry, one of His inner-circle disciples, Peter, denied Him during the greatest trial of His life. Judas, one of the nine, betrayed Him, and at the cross the rest of His disciples left Him except for John. The Twelve were ordinary work-ingmen; none was a priest or politician or rich or famous.

Their immaturity and lack of understanding of Jesus' real purpose in life are revealed by one particular incident recorded in the Bible. The brothers James and John came to Jesus and asked Him, "When You come into Your Kingdom would You grant us the position of sitting on Your right hand and left hand to rule the nation of Israel?"

When the other ten disciples heard about it they were all very upset. Jesus knows the challenge of making disciples with the right attitude, godly character and maturity.

Scripture declares that Jesus had to go through just about every human experience. The Bible says Jesus was tempted in all points just as we are, except He did not yield to any of the temptations. Jesus knew popularity and rejection, success and failure (failure according to man's evaluation). Many stopped following Him at one point, and He was betrayed by one of His own chosen disciples. Jesus saw and experienced the faults and failures of the human race. He experienced His own Jewish race crying out to the Romans, "Crucify Him!"

Jesus was tortured with 39 stripes, ridiculed, mocked, beaten. They placed a crown of thorns on his head. Jesus carried the cross on His lacerated shoulders and down those cobblestone streets on His way to Golgotha, where He was to be crucified. The Roman soldiers nailed his hands and feet to the cross, raised the cross with Jesus nailed to it and dropped it into the hole they had dug to hold it upright.

While Jesus was hanging on the cross in all of His torturous pain and agony, He looked at the Jews and Romans and said, "Father, forgive them for they do not know what they are doing."

Jesus loved His Father God and was so submitted to His will that He was willing to suffer it all for what it would do for the human race. Part of what enabled Him to endure it was the revelation He had—that when He shed His life's blood it would be the price He was paying for the purchase of redeemed humankind.

The apostle Paul tells us to feed the Church that Jesus purchased with His own blood (see Acts 20:28). And the writer of Hebrews explains that Jesus endured the cross, despising the shame, for the joy (the Church) that was set before Him (see Hebrews 12:2).

While we were yet sinners Christ loved us and died for us (see Romans 5:8). He was the life and love of God manifested in the earth (see Hebrews 1:3). He also became the pattern, the type of person God wanted both now and eternally—"according to the eternal purpose which [Father God] accomplished in Christ Jesus our Lord" (Ephesians 3:11).

Jesus Demonstrated True Manhood

Jesus was born into the human race as a mortal man for several reasons: to die on the cross in order to provide redemption for humankind, to reveal to all creation the core motivation for all God does and is—*love*, to purchase the Church with His own blood, to give God the opportunity to father His only biological Son and to experience what it is to be a mortal man and face all the temptations that mortal man faces.

In this book, we are going to major in that last reason: Jesus became a man among the human race, experiencing all the joys, sorrows, tests and challenges of being righteous in a wicked world. Jesus became the Son of man that we might become the sons of God. Jesus died that we might have an abundant life. Jesus came to earth and prepared the way for us to go to heaven. Jesus loved the body that God had made for humans, and He came to earth to obtain a human body that He could live in. Jesus was separated from that body for three days, and then He reentered that body, transforming it into a resurrected immortal human body. Then Jesus sat down at the right hand of the Father in heaven in that body, and He will live in that body forever. (See Romans 1:4; 1 Corinthians 15:1–4; Hebrews 10:12–13.)

Jesus will resurrect and translate all who are His at the end of the mortal Church Age. He will make their bodies glorious bodies like His own. We will all be one united humankind, Church-race family living and working together with Jesus forever and ever (see 1 Thessalonians 5:23).

In the meantime, we have the Law of Transformation and the Process for Conformity to finish here on earth before we graduate to that glorious future of ruling and reigning with our Lord and Savior, Jesus Christ. We will now venture into the following chapters that will explain with Scriptures and life experiences what this is all about and how it works in shaping us into His likeness.

ACKNOWLEDGMENT & PETITION

Father God, I thank You for the revelation that Your highest calling for my life is being conformed to the likeness of Christ Jesus. You confirmed that by having Jesus spend thirty years becoming Your type of man and only three and a half years demonstrating Your ministry to humankind. Help me to align my priorities to Yours. I submit willingly to Your Law of Transformation and Your Process for Conformity making me in Jesus' likeness. I receive the grace from You to go through the processes. I trust in Your promise that You would never allow the Process to be more than I can handle. Thank You, Jesus. I want to be Your person to fulfill Your predestined purpose.

4

God's Inheritance in the Saints

[I pray] that the God of our Lord Jesus Christ, the Father of glory, may give to you the spirit of wisdom and revelation in the knowledge of [Jesus], the eyes of your understanding being enlightened; that you may know . . . what are the riches of the glory of [God's] inheritance in the saints.

Ephesians 1:17–18

There are certain Scriptures that, in just a line or two, convey the foundational truths of our faith. John 3:16, for instance, always comes to mind when we think about salvation, and Acts 2:4 when we think about the gift of the Holy Spirit. Romans 8:29 is one of our key Scriptures in proving that God's highest call for saints is being conformed to Christlikeness: "For whom [God] foreknew, He also predestined to be conformed to the image of

His Son, that [Jesus] might be the firstborn among many brethren."

There are several other verses that convey this truth. Let's continue our exploration by looking at these as a basis for our inheritance in Jesus.

Inheritance—of the Saints and the Father

The Bible speaks of the saints having an inheritance in Christ: "In [Christ] also we have obtained an inheritance" (Ephesians 1:11). Our inheritance is to be children of God with eternal life and to spend eternity with Jesus. Our inheritance is also being joint heirs with Christ Jesus, having access to all things that God the Father has promised and provided for Jesus to be and do.

God the Father also has an inheritance that He is joyfully looking forward to receiving. He is looking for the image and likeness of His Son in the lives of His saints. Personally, I really want God to find He has an inheritance in me on that day when I stand before Him. As the apostle Paul declared, I am pressing toward the mark for the prize of the high calling of God in Christ Jesus, which is being formed in me until I reach the fullness of His likeness (see Philippians 3:14; Ephesians 4:13, 15; Galatians 4:19).

Our Confirmation of Christlikeness

Second Corinthians 3:18 tells us this: "We all, with unveiled face, beholding as in a mirror the glory of the Lord, are being transformed into the same image from glory to glory, just as by the Spirit of the Lord." Glory is the manifest presence of Jesus Christ, the personification of His Person and all that Jesus is in all areas of His life. Jesus is the glory of God just as we are to be the glory of Jesus. Going from glory to glory means we are going from Christlikeness to more Christlikeness until we come to the likeness and maturity of Christ Himself.

The verse that follows says: "Therefore, since we have this ministry . . . we do not lose heart" (2 Corinthians 4:1). What ministry is Paul talking about? The ministry of being conformed to the image of Jesus Christ. When we uncover the process needed to transform us into the glory/likeness of Jesus, you will understand why we do not lose heart by getting discouraged or confused by what is taking place in our lives. We will understand and adjust accordingly. In fact, we will be able to act upon the word Paul gave the Thessalonian Christians who were going through the Process: Rejoice evermore and in all things give thanks.

Jesus Suffered to Make Christlike Sons

Hebrews 2:10 states: "It was fitting for Him, for whom are all things and by whom are all things, in bringing many sons to glory, to make the captain of their salvation perfect through sufferings." Notice that the reason it was fitting for Jesus to go through His sufferings was to bring many sons unto glory/ into the likeness of Christ. Jesus, the perfect man, was made more perfect to be the captain of our salvation through the things He suffered.

Jesus was the brightness of God's glory and the express image of His Father God (see Hebrews 1:3). The glory of God is Jesus Christ whose glory and likeness we are to manifest and become. Jesus said that anyone who has seen Him has seen the Father, for He and His Father are one (see John 14:9).

Strange Is Standard for God's Chosen Ones

Several Scriptures reveal that the Law of Transformation and Process for Conformity that shape us to the character and likeness of Christ require some suffering in the flesh. It is mostly in our emotions and mind, but sometimes it can be in the physical. God's thinking and attitude toward humankind's suffering in the flesh is quite different from humankind's thinking and attitude. God spoke to us through Isaiah the prophet: "'My thoughts are not your thoughts, nor are your ways My ways,' says the LORD. 'For as the heavens are higher than the earth, so are My ways higher than your ways, and My thoughts than your thoughts'" (Isaiah 55:8–9).

Peter said that the fiery trials of our faith are more precious (valuable, costly, honored) than gold. Every trial that is designed to crucify your flesh and conform you more to the likeness of Christ is adding to your gold account in heaven, which represents your desire and willing obedience to be like Jesus.

> Beloved, do not think it strange concerning the fiery trial which is to try you, as though some strange thing happened to you; but rejoice to the extent that you partake of Christ's sufferings, that when His glory is revealed, you may also be glad with exceeding joy.
>
> 1 Peter 4:12–13

The Phillip's translation says it like this:

And now dear friends of mine. I beg you not to be unduly alarmed at the fiery ordeals which come to test your faith, as though this were some abnormal experience. You should be glad, because it means that you are called to share Christ's sufferings. One day, when he shows himself in full splendour to men, you will be filled with the most tremendous joy.

Paul confirms this as well:

For I consider that the sufferings of this present time are not worthy to be compared with the glory [Christlikeness] which shall be revealed in us. For the earnest expectation of the creation eagerly waits for the revealing of the sons of God.

Romans 8:18–9

Peter concludes that it is possible to go through suffering while we are living in the will of God.

Now "If the righteous one is scarcely saved, where will the ungodly and the sinner appear?" Therefore let those who suffer according to the will of God commit their souls to [Jesus] in doing good, as to a faithful Creator.

1 Peter 4:18–19

Jesus Learned Obedience through Suffering

Look at this amazing Scripture:

[Jesus], in the days of His flesh, when He had offered up prayers and supplications, with vehement cries and tears to Him who was able to save Him from death, and was heard because of His godly fear, though He was a Son, yet He learned obedience by the things which He suffered. And having been perfected, He became the author of eternal salvation to all who obey Him.

Hebrews 5:7–9

Jesus prayed and pleaded with great passion and tears for His Father God to save Him from the horrible ordeal of the cross and death. God heard Jesus because of His Son's pure godly fear but did not answer His prayer to save Him from death. Father God knew that this suffering was working together for good for Jesus because His obedience to God's purpose for His life qualified Him to be the author of eternal salvation to all who believe in Him.

The saints who are willing to suffer whatever it takes to fulfill God's purpose for their lives to be conformed to the likeness of His Son will receive the greatest rewards and positions in God's eternal Kingdom. This must be the major reason Paul declared that the sufferings of this present life are not worthy to be compared with the glory that shall be revealed in us.

We Reign with Jesus Only if We Suffer with Him

Romans 8:17 states our purpose clearly: "If [we are] children [of God], then [we are] heirs—heirs of God and joint heirs with Christ, *if indeed we suffer with Him, that we may also be glorified together*" (emphasis added).

Most Christians who quote this verse do not normally include the last line. The privilege of being a joint heir is based on whether or not we have suffered with Jesus. Father God appointed Jesus heir of all things because He was obedient even to death on the cross (see Hebrews 1:2). God's promises of saints ruling and reigning with Christ are based on two things: being conformed to the image of Christ and being an overcomer, for "he who overcomes shall inherit all things" (Revelation 21:7). The rewards that Jesus promised to give to each of the seven churches listed in Revelation 2–3 were given only to those who had proven to be overcomers: "To him who overcomes, I will give . . . ."

We read as well that "if we endure [with Christ], we shall also reign with Him" (2 Timothy 2:12) and "since Christ suffered for us in the flesh, arm yourselves also with the same mind, for he who has suffered in the flesh has ceased from sin" (1 Peter 4:1). The most common suffering in the flesh is crucifying the flesh to allow the life of Christ to be manifest in our bodies.

Paul gives us encouragement for perseverance as we face suffering.

> We have this treasure in earthen vessels, that the excellence of the power may be of God and not of us. We are hard-pressed on every side, yet not crushed; we are perplexed, but not in despair; persecuted, but not forsaken; struck down, but not destroyed—always carrying about in the body the dying of the Lord Jesus, that the life of Jesus also may be manifested in our body. For we who live are always delivered to death for Jesus' sake, that the life of Jesus also may be manifested in our mortal flesh.
>
> 2 Corinthians 4:7–11

Paul is revealing that all our pressures and circumstances are happening in our lives and ministries to cause more and more of the life of Jesus to be made manifest in our mortal bodies. All these things are working for us to transform us into living the life of Christ, which continually conforms us into the likeness of Christ. Paul always emphasizes that this is accomplished not by self-effort or dead religious works but by the Holy Spirit working in us, with us and through us. We must come to the place where we can say from experience: "I have been crucified with Christ; it is no longer I who live, but Christ lives in me; and the life which I now live in the flesh I live by the faith in the Son of God, who loved me and gave Himself for me" (Galatians 2:20).

We must come to the place that we continually crucify the carnal selfish life and allow the life of Christ to be our motivation and desired way of living. Since most Christians have not attained the likeness of Christ, God puts them through the processes required for transforming them into their highest callings according to His eternal purpose.

In the words of Jesus, "Whoever desires to come after Me, *let him deny himself, and take up his cross, and follow Me.* For whoever desires to save his life will lose it, but whoever loses his life for My sake and the gospel's will save it" (Mark 8:34–35, emphasis added). Our personal cross is denial to our self-life and submission to the life of Christ. We should do this to reach our highest calling, but also because Jesus said that unless we do so, we cannot be His disciples.

Eight Reasons for Fulfilling God's Highest Calling

Let's read again God's highest priority and greatest purpose for humankind: It is for us to become fully the likeness of

Jesus Christ, to be conformed to His nature and character in all areas.

There are eight major reasons that God wants this calling to be fulfilled. These are greater than and different from what most Christians expect them to be. God's way of thinking about the human race is higher than ours, just as the heavens are higher than the earth.

I give you here the eight major reasons for which God created humankind on earth. We have discussed a few of these. Several of them have been accomplished in the history of humankind, but others are still in the process of being fulfilled.

The First Reason

God created humankind in His image and likeness to fill the earth with a human race in His likeness. The first part of that purpose is fulfilled, but Jesus is still working on the second part.

The Second Reason

God created humankind in order to demonstrate His nature and character of love. This purpose was fulfilled at Calvary where Jesus demonstrated God's love.

The Third Reason

God created humankind with free moral agency so that they could be tested and purified until conformed to the image of Christ. The first half has been done, but the second part is still taking place.

The Fourth Reason

God created humankind with the power to procreate in order to fulfill His eternal Fatherhood by fathering His own biological Son. This was fulfilled when God overshadowed Mary with His procreative power, making her pregnant with Jesus Christ, who became the only begotten Son of God.

The Fifth Reason

God created humankind in order to provide a many-membered Bride for His Son. Jesus became a mortal human so that He could shed His life-blood on the cross to purchase His Bride, a body of redeemed humankind. This purpose has been fulfilled, but the Holy Spirit is still working to complete the Bride.

The Sixth Reason

God created humankind in order to birth the Church—the Body of Christ on earth—as joint heirs who co-labor with Him in carrying out God's eternal purpose. This purpose is close to being finished. Just a few more million saints need to be added to the Body to make it complete and brought to maturity. The Church also must demonstrate the Kingdom of God in every nation until every nation on earth becomes a "goat" or "sheep" nation.

The Seventh Reason

God created humankind to be a praise to His glory and worship Him in spirit and in truth.

The Eighth Reason

God created humankind to fellowship with Him as a comparable and compatible fellow being. Too many Christians think of God as being a lonely old man in the universe with no one for fellowship, so He created humans, and He needs humankind so much that He welcomes anyone who will come and be with Him. Many see Jesus as just a big jolly Santa Claus who loves everyone so much that He will let anyone into heaven who wants to enter. We will discover more about who God really is and His attitude toward us as He works to bring His purpose to fruition.

ACKNOWLEDGMENT & PETITION

Jesus, Your Word declares that I have an inheritance in You, and it is glorious in this life and much more abundant in Your eternal Kingdom. I appreciate it and am determined to appropriate all You want me to possess and manifest in this life. I passionately want You to find Your inheritance in me to Your satisfaction—for my life to be conformed to Your image and likeness as it was fully manifested in Your life. You and I have made a covenant together as You and Abraham did. If I have passed my tests, as Abraham did, then let my prophetic promises be changed to a sworn oath. Thank You, Lord, together forever! Amen.

5

The Higher the Calling, the Greater the Testing Process

The LORD tests the righteous. . . . God tested Abraham. . . . The genuineness of your faith [is] much more precious than gold that perishes, though it is tested by fire.

Psalm 11:5; Genesis 22:1; 1 Peter 1:7

There are many men of God in the Bible who portray the truth that the higher the calling, the greater the testing process will be. The following portray it the most: Abraham, Moses, Job, Joseph, David, Jeremiah, Paul and the man Christ Jesus. We have covered much of the trials and sufferings that Jesus went through while He was a mortal man on earth. The sufferings of Jesus were not only redemptive for others, but they also gained Him a name above all other names in heaven and earth.

One of the great positions that His suffering promoted Him to was being the Head of the Church. He was given that position because He shed His blood to the point of dying on the cross, which purchased His Church. The Church would be like a Bride to Him and would be joined with Him to co-labor and reign together forever.

We noted that Hebrews 12:2 reveals some of what helped Jesus go through the sufferings on the cross: Jesus, for the *joy* set before Him, endured the cross, despising the shame. What was the joy set before Jesus that enabled Him to endure the shame and suffering? It was the purchasing of the Church, which He had planned from the foundation of the world. Jesus loved the Church and gave Himself for her. Jesus was slain on the cross in the mind and purpose of God before the world was founded. Revelation 13:8 tells us that "the Lamb [was] slain from the foundation of the world." Father God chose us, the Church, in Christ and for Christ, before the foundation of the world (see Ephesians 1:4; 5:25).

Great Suffering Brings Great Rewards

I bring these Scriptures to your attention to let you know that any suffering God has for us to go through to produce the likeness and maturity of Christ in us will be so greatly rewarded that we will exclaim with Paul that the sufferings of this earthly life are not worthy to be compared to the glory that shall be revealed in us and the positional awards that we will receive.

Paul suffered more than most of the first-century Christian ministers. He is also the author of fourteen of the 27 books in the New Testament. God demonstrated how much he honored Paul by choosing fourteen of his writings to be books of inspired Scripture. This is twice as many as were chosen from the writings of all twelve of the personal apostles of Jesus Christ. Jesus loved the revelation and teaching of Paul because he had the most complete revelation regarding the Church. You would think that the Twelve would have the most revelation, for they walked and talked personally with Jesus for over three years.

I have found in my many years of ministry that those who have heavenly visitations, those who walk and talk with Jesus in heaven, do not have any more revelation of Christ's Church than those who receive truth by the spirit of wisdom and revelation. Nor do they have any greater understanding of God's purpose for the Church, why God created man or God's highest calling for man.

In my earlier years of ministry, I heard testimonies about people having visions, visits to heaven, angelic visitations, etc. I fasted, prayed and cried out to God to let me experience those things.

God spoke to me one day and reminded me that He had called me like David. My life and ministry would be similar to his life and ministry. I would go through some of the experiences David went through and help do for the Kingdom of God what David did for the kingdom of Israel.

I researched the life of David and found he had no out-of-body experiences like the prophet Ezekiel, yet the Bible calls David a prophet. David had no angelic visitations, where angels talked to him and gave him revelation and instruction, as Abraham experienced and some of the other prophets. There was very little of the supernatural in his life except for the supernatural prophetic and some angelic help in some of his battles. He received many personal prophecies, and he wrote with prophetic inspiration, such as some of the prophetic psalms about the coming Messiah (see Psalm 22:1, 14, 16). David prayed the very words that Jesus said while hanging on the cross: "My God, My God, why have You forsaken Me?" (Mark 15:34).

Many of his prayers actually describe what they did to Jesus on the cross: "They pierced my hands and my feet." Jesus said the psalms spoke of Him, and many of the writers of the New Testament quoted phrases from David's psalms to prove their New Testament teachings. I taught the book of Psalms in Bible college and discovered many words that Christ was praying through David. We concluded that the things Jesus prayed when He went to the mountain alone and prayed all night could be found in the psalms.

Experiences That Expand

The same was true for me when I started moving in the prophetic in 1953, and again in 1973 when I received a divine visitation that anointed and enabled me to minister personal prophecies to 85 saints on one January night. The prophesying continued from ten at night till two in the morning. As I mentioned earlier, over the next 25 years I gave personal prophecies to more than fifty thousand individuals. God gave a reproducing anointing that enabled our ministry, Christian International, to teach, activate and train more than half a million of God's people in the supernatural prophetic ministry all over the world.

I am sharing this with you to reveal that we did all of this without unusual supernatural manifestations but with God's giftings, grace and the faith to act on His word. That is mainly because God called me as a prophet like David instead of like Ezekiel. I was granted revelation and anointing to teach and activate people into the supernatural prophetic ministry, but I have not received the revelation and anointing to activate visions, dreams, angelic visitations or out-of-body experiences.

My daughter-in-law, Jane Hamon, has written a book on dreams and visions and conducts seminars teaching and training saints how to receive dreams and visions and to interpret them. The people who sit under her teaching and anointing start receiving more dreams and visions. Maybe it works the way it did with Peter and John and the lame man: "Such as I have I give to you!" Maybe there is a divine principle that if you have a special anointing you can give it to others for their benefit and for impartation of that same experience and anointing.

One of my spiritual sons, Guillermo Maldonado, has an anointing and gifting for healings and miracles. I have been in big stadium meetings with him. He will pray a corporate prayer for healing and miracles, and hundreds of people will then form a long line to give testimonies of miraculous healing. The pastors who come under his ministry also begin to experience miracles in their services, and their churches grow. Many of those who sit under Kenneth Copeland's teaching and anointing of faith, prosperity and victorious living receive and manifest the same.

Our Majors and Minors in Ministry

I have had a few spiritual dreams and visions since the first time I went to the altar. I saw Jesus hanging on the cross and saying to me, "I gave My life for you; will you give your life to Me?" I got saved on my sixteenth birthday on July 29, 1950.

In the early 1990s, Cindy Jacobs prophesied to me that God had made me a five-star general in the army of the Lord. That was the time that God had me start doing corporate spiritual warfare in the nations. In 1997 I received a vision with three different scenes. In one of the scenes Jesus introduced me to the archangel Michael, the top general in God's heavenly army of war angels.

In the vision Jesus said to Michael, "This is Bill Hamon, a major general in God's army of warrior saints on earth." After Jesus left us, we talked for some time about how our two armies would work together, with Jesus our Commander in Chief, to prepare the way for Jesus' return and to make the kingdoms of this world the Kingdom of Jesus and His anointed Church, which is destined to rule and reign with Him over the new earth (see 2 Peter 3:13; Revelation 5:10).

Paul and the Spirit of Wisdom and Revelation

Paul wrote in the book of Ephesians that God revealed to him the mystery of the Church. He gives several reasons why Jesus wanted the Church and the many things it was to accomplish for God. Paul wrote that the Church consisted of many members, which he called the Body of Christ. The Church is the new creation of humankind, those who have been born again into a new creation in Christ. (See Ephesians 3:5; 1 Corinthians 12:12, 27.)

It is no longer like God's dispensation of the Law. Abraham was chosen by God to raise up a special Hebrew race that would later be called the Israelis/Jews and would become known as the people of the God of heaven and earth. In those days a person had to become a member of the Israeli religion to join the people of the Most High God. Jesus came about fifteen hundred years after Joshua and the Israeli army had by military warfare removed condemned nations from the land of Canaan and made it the land and nation of Israel.

Now in the Church Age, Jesus has made the way for whoever in the human race wants to become a child of the Most High God. In the Church, Jew and Gentile have become one new creation in Christ.

Most of what we know about the Church's structure, function and purpose comes from the writings of the apostle Paul. He brought the revelation of our highest calling. The reason I am sharing so much about the apostle Paul is because he is the one who wrote our key Scripture text and the main one we are using as an example of Christians suffering for Christ.

Some of Paul's Challenges

Some self-appointed apostles started going to some of the churches that Paul had established. They tried to make themselves great by telling some of the things they had gone through to preach the Gospel. They were creating confusion and improperly taking offerings and mistreating the saints. Paul felt he had to counter what they were doing by letting the Corinthian church know what he had suffered for preaching the Gospel. I believe he felt self-conscious about revealing his experiences, but he felt it was necessary to expose these false apostles to the Corinthian church members.

Here is a list of some of the things Paul suffered for Jesus and the Gospel, taken from 2 Corinthians 11:22–33.

1. Abundant labors
2. Frequent imprisonment
3. Whipped numerous times
4. Five times beaten with 39 stripes
5. Three times beaten with rods
6. Three times shipwrecked
7. A day and a night in the depths of the sea
8. Traveled many miles facing dangers from flooded rivers, robbers, persecution from the Jews and at the hands of the Gentiles
9. Faced grave dangers from mobs in the cities (He was stoned to death, but God raised him back to life again.)
10. Persecuted by men who claimed to be brothers in Christ but were not
11. Faced death in deserts and on stormy seas (including a fourteen-day storm at sea)
12. Lived with weariness, pain, hunger, thirst and sleepless nights
13. Shivered with coldness
14. Had constant concern for how the churches were coming along
15. Was let down over a wall in a basket to escape Damascus
16. Had to confront some false apostles who were deceitful workers, transforming themselves into apostles of

Christ and deceiving the churches (And no wonder! For Satan transforms himself into an angel of light; therefore, it is no great thing if his ministers also transform themselves into ministers of righteousness, whose end will be according to their works.)

Paul was in prison when he was launched to heaven by being beheaded by the Romans. Keep in mind as we study God's process for conforming us to the image and likeness of Jesus Christ that the majority of Scriptures we will use were written by Paul.

The Apostle of Our Text

Paul is the apostle who wrote Romans 8:28–29, our key proof Scripture. Paul declared: "We know that all things work together for good to those who love God and to those who are called according to His purpose. . . ."

When Paul says, "we know" or "I know," he is not talking about knowledge from a book or something someone taught him. No, he is saying, "I have experienced many horrible things, things that did not make any logical sense at the time. But by revelation from God, I discovered this tremendous truth. If I love God and am called according to God's purpose, then all things must work together for my good."

Think of all the things that happened to Paul. And yet he can say he knew it was all working together for his good. How could that possibly be? Could all the things that he suffered somehow have been working together for his good?

And what is the "good" that all things are working together to produce? It is what God predestined. For Paul to be conformed to the likeness of His Son is what all things were working together to accomplish. All things are not working together to produce a more comfortable lifestyle with everything happening as we think it should. All things are working together to fulfill God's highest calling in our lives. We need to know that God is out to kill our old nature so that our new nature created in Christ Jesus may be in control and we can live the life of Christ.

Beginning to Learn in the Process

I remember a time in 1972 when I was facing a heartbreaking, mind-blowing situation. I had just gone through a similar situation a few years before. I was praying, moaning and crying.

Thirty minutes into my crying prayer, I said, "God, I can't go through this again. It's not fair or right. It's killing me. It's killing me!"

I suddenly heard the Holy Spirit in me talking to God in a laughing tone, saying, "Father, it's working; it's working!"

I thought to myself, *What is the Holy Spirit talking about? What is working?*

And then I knew. When I said, "It's killing me," the Holy Spirit knew that that was what the trauma I was going through was supposed to do: kill that part of me that was not Christlike and transform that part of my life to function like Christ's nature. At that time, I had no idea that was just one small part of the Process for Conformity to Christ, the Law of Transformation being applied. It was like one piece of a large jigsaw puzzle that had to be put together over the next 47 years and more.

I will share many more life experiences to illustrate how the Process for Conformity and the Law of Transformation work in the Church. Every saint who is predestined by Father God to be transformed into Christ's likeness will go through the conformity process according to God's own choice for each saint.

After 85 years of being on this earth, 70 years of being a Christian and 66 years of being a minister, I hope that there are only one or two pieces of the jigsaw puzzle left to make the picture of my conformity to the likeness of Christ complete.

Two Vital Verses for Our Understanding

Thank God Paul put the truth in Romans 8:28 before he revealed God's highest calling and purpose for creating humankind on earth in verse 29! All Christians should memorize these two verses. They are vital in understanding God's purpose for our lives on earth.

Many people over the years would ask my wife and me, "How have you made it all these years of pioneering? You were preaching about the restoration of prophets and apostles in the 1970s when most of the Church did not believe there were apostles and prophets in the twentieth-century Church."

We would always share with them Romans 8:28–29. We kept going during the darkest and most hopeless times by keeping the eternal in view and not just the present situation. We had the revelation that all things had to be working together for our good—not just to make us greater and more successful ministers at the present time, but to put us through the Process of developing His highest calling for our lives, conforming us through His Process more and more into Christ's likeness. We had to submit to the Holy Spirit's ministry through the Law of Transformation before we could advance to our increased ministry of demonstration.

God's priority is more on making the man than making the ministry. We will not be taking our great ministries to heaven, and the Christian entrepreneur who was successful enough to give millions to further the Church will not be taking the business to heaven with him or her. All we will stand before God with is our "self." If you do not begin to understand God's process for perfecting us in Christ's likeness, then you will become confused and very discouraged when God's time comes for you to be tested, tried and purified for a higher level of Christlikeness. In my "10 M's" for determining a true minister, the "M" of manhood is the most important (see the list at the end of this book).

Tested Like Gold, Tried by Fire

There are several passages in the Bible that tell us God tests the righteous. There are also biblical examples of God testing His special chosen ones. We have already mentioned Abraham. Genesis 22 tells us that "God tested Abraham" by asking him to take his only son whom he greatly loved and go to a certain mountain and offer him to the Lord as a human sacrifice.

I am always amazed at Abraham's faith and willingness to fulfill God's command immediately. It was his greatest trial for two reasons. First, it was a heartbreaking thought to him as a father. Second, it was illogical, for it would cancel all of God's prophecies to him. God had rejected Abraham's son, Ishmael, by an Egyptian woman. He had supernaturally enabled Sarah to get pregnant and birth a son, Isaac, when she was ninety and Abraham was one hundred.

This was the last chance for God's promises to Abraham to be fulfilled because they were all wrapped up in Isaac. Now God was telling Abraham to take his only son, whom he deeply loved, and kill him and burn him on the altar of sacrifice. Why would God ask him to do such an unreasonable and illogical thing when it had required so much to get to this place? If you receive the revelation of God's purpose for all the things that happen in your life, it will take the "why" out of your conversation.

Why No More "Why"?

Just a couple of months ago, as of this writing, the Tollesons, a husband and wife who have been with our Christian International Apostolic Network (CIAN) ministerial association for more than 25 years, attended one of my Mentoring Days, during which I taught these principles. Rodney, the husband, has been assisting in my Mentoring Day meetings, but his wife, Cathy, had not participated until then. She attended all the sessions and really got the understanding of why we do not say "why"—why we choose not to question God for allowing certain things to happen to us.

Two weeks after they arrived back at their home in Florida, they received the medical report back from a number of tests on Rodney. It revealed he had pancreatic cancer.

When Cathy read that, she thought about how they had been ministers for Jesus for 25 years, faithfully served God and even ate very healthy foods, and yet Rodney got pancreatic cancer. She started to utter the words *God, why?*, but before they came out of her mouth, she stopped the words from being spoken. Instead, she refused to waste her time asking a nonprofitable question that would only stir up confusion, sadness, despair and feelings of hopelessness. Instead she remembered the teaching that all things must work together for good to those who love God and are called according to His purpose.

They declared that they were not going to waste their time on analyzing how and why this happened. They decided to put away all confusion and consecrate all their time, energy and thoughts on practicing the biblical principles of healing and restoration, whether naturally or supernaturally or a combination of both.

They decided to follow Abraham's example and have faith in God's wisdom, power and faithfulness and not be concerned about the "why" of it all.

Somehow Abraham had such faith that he did not question why God would ask him to do such a thing as to kill his son. He had no written material that explained God and His ways of doing things, for he lived five hundred years before Moses wrote the laws of God in a book. We can see why the New Testament calls Abraham the father of God's people of faith. Abraham had no way of knowing that God was going to use his experience as an illustration to His new race of people to teach them what faith is and how it works to justify us before God (see Romans 4).

It would also be two thousand years before Paul would write about Abraham to the Roman church to illustrate faith. This is true concerning most of the patriarchs in the Bible.

Paul declared that all the experiences that the children of Israel went through in their journey from Egypt happened and were documented for our admonition and learning. How do we know if the trials and tests we go through may illustrate to others how to go through suffering victoriously (see 1 Corinthians 10:11)?

Look at Job. We have hope and encouragement when we go through heartbreaking, mind-blowing loss by remembering the story of Job in the Bible. It all worked together for his good by delivering him from his fear and self-importance. (In Job 29, the words *I, me* and *my* appear 29 times in 25 verses. Compare this to Romans 7, the "self" chapter—*I, me, my, myself* occur fifty times in 25 verses.) Job was transformed from *self*-centered to *God*-centered. God then gave him back double all he had lost (see Job 42:10).

Abraham's Seventh Major Test—and Mine

When I taught the book of Genesis for five years in Bible college, we discovered that Abraham went through seven major tests; this one challenging him to sacrifice his son was number seven. During my early years of ministry God spoke to me that my life and ministry would be like Abraham's in that I would be a pioneer and the father of many.

In spring 2014 I was wondering, after sixty years of ministry, if I had gone through my seventh and final major test like Abraham. I knew I had gone through at least six major tests, but what about the seventh?

A few days later God asked me if I was ready for Genesis 22:1, which would be my seventh and final major test. I knew

God was not thinking about taking one of my three children, but my wife. It was a challenging question.

As I meditated on how to answer Him, it came to my mind how I had been preaching about the truth that God is always a good God and whatever He decides to do is the best. In teaching the historical books of the Bible, I led the class in a thorough study of the story of Isaiah prophesying to King Hezekiah that he was to set his house in order, for he was about to die. The prophet left and Hezekiah attempted a plea bargain with God. He reminded God what a great reformer he had been in restoring Israel back to true worship. He was age 39 at the time and felt that he was way too young to die. God sent the prophet back to tell the king he had fifteen more years to live on earth.

During those extra fifteen years granted to King Hezekiah, ten major evil things happened. The most serious was Manasseh being born. He became king after Hezekiah died and reigned for 55 years. He was so evil and committed so many atrocities against God, the Temple and all Israel that God decreed Israel was going into captivity and no one was going to talk Him out of it.

It Is Best to Leave Things to God

This example taught me that it is not wise to talk God out of doing something He wants to happen or has already spoken will happen. That is the reason that when God asked me to sacrifice my wife, Evelyn, to Him by her coming to heaven, I did not try to talk Him out of it. Father God requests nothing and does nothing that is not best for His children's eternal good.

I did reason some with God. "Lord, You know I love Evelyn. She has been such a faithful and helpful wife to me for 59 years. She has been such a good co-laborer with me and helped bring the ministry to become the worldwide influence that it is today. She is known as Mom Hamon to tens of thousands around the world. We all have been praying for a miracle of healing and restoration to her body, for she has suffered much over the last few years. But, God, You said it is Your will and time for her to come home to her heavenly Father."

That finalized it for me. If it was God's will and time for her to go home to Jesus, then I must and would submit to God's will without any further debate about it. I kept encouraging her to do what she could to get better. She would just say for me not to worry; she was ready to go and felt it was her time.

Jesus appeared to her in her bedroom. She said He stretched out His hand toward her and smiled really lovingly. I asked her if she felt as if He were reassuring her that she was going to be healed, or was Jesus inviting and welcoming her home? She said she did not know, but she had no desire to stay after that. She went on to be with the Lord on September 22, 2014, at age 77.

Christian International had planned a great event to celebrate my "80–60" at our annual International Gathering of Apostles and Prophets (IGAP) conference in October 2014. That was my eighty years of living and sixty years of ministry. She left a month before the great celebration, with more than five hundred attending the banquet. But we all knew Evelyn was celebrating her homecoming with greater joy and excitement beyond our imagination.

People would ask me, "How did you adjust to losing your wife after 59 years of marriage?

I would reply that instead of thinking about my loss and loneliness I would meditate on how happy and fulfilled she is now that she is in heaven. She is enjoying a body that does not have any sickness or pain, not one extra pound of fat, no wrinkles and a peace in her spirit and joy unspeakable in her soul. She is young and even more beautiful than when I married her when she was eighteen.

I have said jokingly to some of my friends, "You know what happened? After 59 years of marriage a man came by . . . smiled lovingly at my wife . . . stretched out His hand toward her . . . and she just took off with Him!" In all seriousness I am glad it was Jesus, for I know that I will join them some day in the future. I thank God that, because of the revelation of God's highest calling, there is no "why" left in the situation, only peace and full assurance.

It Works for All, in All Kinds of Situations

One member of my board of governors lost his wife in a car accident a few months after my wife went to heaven. It was unexpected and sudden; no one had any idea that she would be in heaven that soon. I shared with him the truth of the Law of Transformation. He had no problem with the "why" of the whole thing. I find this truth works in all situations of life. That is one reason I am writing this book—so everyone who reads it can have this truth as a guiding light as he or she walks through the darkness while going through God's Process for Conformity (see Psalm 23:4).

ACKNOWLEDGMENT & PETITION

The great heroes of the Bible, especially Jesus Christ, gave up much to fulfill their callings. The apostle Paul is the one who suffered the most and wrote the most about God's purpose in suffering, tests and trials. Since all Scripture is given by the inspiration of God, I believe that Romans 8:28–29 is as true and workable as John 3:16. All things are working together for my conformity to the likeness of Jesus Christ. Thank You, Lord, for Your encouraging assurance that the greater the Process for Conformity, the greater the reward—of being with You and co-laboring together forever and ever. Amen!

6

How the Process Works!

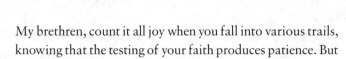

My brethren, count it all joy when you fall into various trails,
knowing that the testing of your faith produces patience. But
let patience have its perfect work, that you may be perfect
[Christlike] and complete, lacking nothing.

James 1:2–4

We have now come to the place to explain how
Romans 8:28 works in fulfilling Romans 8:29.
Paul declared that he knew beyond a shadow of
a doubt that when you love God and are called according
to God's purpose then all things do work together for your
good to fulfill God's eternal purpose in your life. That purpose and highest calling for now and eternity is saints being
conformed to Christ's likeness and character—in all areas
of life. Everything that happens in the life of a true Christian is relegated and directed according to God's priority as
revealed in Romans 8:28–29.

Requirements for Working

The reason I say a *true Christian* is because there are two requirements for Romans 8:28 to work.

First, you must love God with all your heart, soul, mind and strength, which Jesus said is the first and greatest Commandment. The way you prove and demonstrate your love for God is by keeping the commandments of Jesus, and loving Him is the first one. Jesus gave many commandments in the four gospels and the other New Testament books for true Christians to practice. When the Bible speaks of "loving God" it is not referring just to worshiping Jesus with joy and devotion; it includes keeping all the commandments of Jesus.

Second, the "calling" is according to His purpose of conformity to Jesus Christ and not our grandiose ideas and visions of being called to have the most glorious and spectacular life and ministry (see 1 John 5:3; 2 John 1:6).

Pressing toward the Goal

The challenge of the Law of Transformation and the Process for Conformity is decentralizing man from his carnal, selfish, natural self-life, and then conforming that self-life to the life of Christ. The moment Eve let her self-desire overrule God's command not to eat the fruit, "self" became the main restriction to humankind's being in God's likeness. From the moment we were born, we were babied to be selfish and self-centered. Everybody took care of us. We could do nothing for ourselves. If we needed our pants changed or were hungry, someone came immediately and took care of us. We could not walk or talk. If they did not come immediately, we cried out a pitiful or angry cry, then everyone came running to meet our needs. We could not formulate words to communicate with those around us.

Basically, we were helpless—and, in a way, useless. All babies are good for is for Mom and all the family to have someone to adore, love and take care of. Babies subconsciously get the impression that everybody and everything around them is to fulfill their desires and needs. Sad to say, some people never grow out of that impression. But for those who love God and are the called, they are the ones destined to be decentralized by the Law of Transformation and to grow through the conforming Process.

When teaching a CI course on pitfalls in the prophetic, I show the students a drawing of a large fruit tree with three big limbs growing out and up from the trunk of the tree and branches growing out with every type of evil fruit on it. The three big limbs represent the *lust of the flesh*, the *lust of the eyes* and the *pride of life*. The devil has used these three to tempt humankind since he used them to tempt Eve in the Garden of Eden. The devil used the same three on Jesus during the wilderness temptation. The fruit on the tree represents all the sins of the world. The taproot that supplies the tree with what it needs to function is not the devil or the world but *self*. The devil or the world with the three major instruments of temptation cannot wrongly motivate the mind or body of humans to sin when the self-life is truly crucified with Christ, dead to sin and hidden with Christ in God (see Romans 6:6–14; Colossians 3:1–4, 10).

Jesus has given us power over the devil (see Luke 10:19) and the grace to resist temptation, but our degree of victorious

Christian living depends on how much we have been transformed and conformed to the nature and mature character of Jesus Christ. Being born again to a new creation in Christ Jesus happens in a moment's time, and when our bodies are changed into immortality it will happen in the twinkling of an eye, but it requires most of our lives to be transformed and matured into the likeness of Jesus Christ.

That is the reason we can say, "I have been redeemed in my spirit, I am being redeemed in my soul, and I shall be redeemed in my body." God wants us to have a full redemption of spirit, soul and body (see 1 Thessalonians 5:23). Paul declared at the end of his days, "I do not count myself to have obtained perfection/conformity to Christlikeness, but I am pressing toward that goal for the prize of the highest calling of God in Christ Jesus, having been conformed to His likeness" (see Philippians 3:13–14).

Being Processed by My "Friends"

James 1:2–5 talks about our "friends" who work for our benefit in conforming the self-life to the Christ-life. In the early 1950s *Letters to Young Churches* came into my possession. It was J. B. Phillips's first paraphrase of the New Testament epistles from Greek into modern English. I memorized this passage and have quoted it hundreds of times in the course of my ministry. It reveals the truth about our "friends" whom God has appointed to help conform us to Christlikeness.

When all kinds of *trials and temptations* crowd into your lives my brothers, don't resent them as intruders, but welcome

98

them *as friends*! Realise that they come to test your faith and to produce in you the quality of endurance. But let the process go on until that endurance is fully developed, and you will find you have become men of mature character with the right sort of independence. And if, in the process, any of you does not know how to meet any particular problem he has only to ask God—who gives generously to all men without making them feel foolish or guilty—and he may be quite sure that the necessary wisdom will be given him.

James 1:2–5 PHILLIPS, emphasis added

This word from God through the writings of James declares that *tests, temptations and trials are our friends to kill our carnal self-life and transform us into the integrity and mature character of Jesus.* Now you know you have more friends than you thought you had! From God's point of view and purpose all our *trials and tests* are our *friends* helping us to be like Jesus.

When I speak this truth to an audience they usually respond with a surprised and challenged laugh, like, *Really? You can't be serious!* But by the time I give them several Scriptures along with biblical and personal examples, what seemed to them like a negative turns into a positive. We are not to resist and resent our trials and tests but welcome them.

Some people have said, "Well, I can welcome some tests, but others I cannot." God says for us to welcome all kinds of trials. The New King James Version says, "Count it all joy when you fall into various trials." *The Message* says, "Consider it a sheer gift, friends, when tests and challenges come at you from all sides." The Amplified says, "Consider it wholly joyful, my brethren, whenever you are enveloped in or encounter trials of any sort." You can check all the Bible translations, and they reveal the same truth but use different expressions.

A Lesson from Personal Experience

When I got married, I inherited a mother-in-law. When I was a single pastor she and I got along. She was quite spiritual. In church services, she would give messages in tongues, and I would give the interpretation. We worked together in casting devils out of people. Since she had been a Christian most of her 39 years and I had been a Christian for only five of my 21 years, she felt it was her duty to mentor me and help me pastor. I would win young people to the Lord, and she would try to straighten them out, and they would get offended and leave.

Even after I became her son-in-law, she was continually correcting me on what I should do and how I should do it. She talked love, gentleness and goodness. I talked faith, fire and power. It came to a place where she was frustrating me to no end. My wife continually had to be the peacemaker between her mother and her husband.

I finally became desperate enough that I went on a three-day fast and prayed much about the matter. At the end of the three days, God spoke to me and said, *You seem to have a problem with your mother-in-law.*

I said, "Yes, she is driving me to frustration and hindering my pastoring. I know she loves You and is spiritual, but You need to change that woman."

Jesus said, *I understand.*

(I thought, No, *You don't, because You never had a mother-in-law to deal with!*)

He went on. *So, you two are different and are frustrating each other, right? Do you want Me to make you like her or her like you so you can live and work together?*

"Lord," I cried, "please don't make me like her, but her like me, maybe?"

Jesus said, *Since that would not work, let Me give you a truth that will work, and it will also conform you to be more like Me. Plus it will give you some wisdom that will help you the rest of your life and ministry. I want you to do this: Give her the right to be herself.*

"But, Lord," I argued, "she is not right in the way she does things."

Whoever she is and whatever she does, give her the right to be and do that.

"Okay, Lord, if that is Your wisdom and answer to my problem, then You give me the grace and wisdom, and I will do it!"

Over the next month I quit trying to adjust her, and I was not getting as frustrated. But she did not change. She kept acting the same way toward me.

I complained again to the Lord.

He said quite sternly, *Bill Hamon, do you really want complete victory and not just partial?*

"Oh yes, Lord!"

Then the Lord said, *This is what I want you to do: Give her the right not to give you the right to be yourself.*

"Lord," I said, "are You serious?"

Yes. If you will let this become part of your nature and way of life, it will help you in dealing with all kinds of people for the rest of your life.

Jesus was right. It has helped me in my marriage, raising my children, working with my staff and board of governors and being bishop to more than four thousand ministers in our Christian International Apostolic Network. When we yield to the Law of Transformation and the Process for Conformity, not only does it make us more like Jesus, but it also makes us more successful in this life.

God Tests His Righteous Children

Psalm 11:5 says that God tests the righteous. He does not test the wicked, for the rest of that verse says that God's soul hates them. The wicked are dead in their trespasses and sin. A farmer does not prune his dead fruit trees; he removes them. But he does prune the living fruit-bearing trees.

Jesus says in John 15:1–2, "I am the true vine, and My Father is the vinedresser. Every branch in Me that does not bear fruit He takes away; and every branch that bears fruit He prunes, that it may bear more fruit."

God only tests and works on perfecting His own righteous children, whom He chastens and adjusts with trials and tests. *Whom the Lord loves* He chastens, tests and tries (see Hebrews 12:6–7). God loves the saints and has chosen them for His friends. They are to fulfill His special purposes. And those saints who have a higher calling require the most intense training. It is like having an elite group of soldiers—such as the special operations command in the Marines. All Marines go through basic training, but these soldiers go through more rigorous and intense training. There are basic things God wants worked into every Christian, but those who have the higher calling require much more.

The Lesson from the Seasons

My wife wrote two booklets that help us understand this concept. One teaches about the four spiritual seasons of life: spring, summer, fall and winter. All Christians go through all four of those seasons in different stages of their lives. If you live in the Deep South of the United States or in a tropical nation, you may not fully relate to the four seasons of nature, but you can understand the concept.

Evelyn usually used parables in her teaching. To portray this truth, she used the illustration of being a young peach tree in the Master's orchard. *Spring* is when everything in your life is coming alive, turning green and blossoming. Your future looks bright and encouraging. *Summer* is when the weather is warm and sunny. Fruit is on your tree, and you feel you are fruitful and advancing in your life and profession. *Fall* is when you begin to see and sense something is changing. The fruit has been picked from your tree, and now the leaves are beginning to fall off. The atmosphere is beginning to cool. You don't feel God's presence as much. Things around you are not as friendly and cooperative. The sap in your tree is descending into the roots of the tree, preparing for the winter season.

Winter is the testing and trying of your faith. In the middle of the winter season, you have no productivity, no fruit, not even leaves. Nothing seems to be working. You feel forsaken, cold and all alone. The temperature drops below freezing, and you have icicles hanging off your limbs.

You wonder, *What's happening to me?* You come to the place where you are saying, "God, I can't take this anymore!"

Then you see the farmer coming with his pruning shears. He begins to prune away some of your barren limbs. You think, *I worked so hard to produce all these limbs. Why are you cutting some of them back and removing others?*

The little peach tree does not realize that all of this is working together for its good. If the tree is properly pruned, it will bear bigger, tastier and better fruit, which will cause more people to want to eat from this tree. The peach tree does not realize that every tree must be pruned each year for maturing and producing bigger and better fruit. It cannot be pruned during the summer when the sap is flowing freely through the limbs. The farmer must wait until the winter season when most of the sap has gone down into the roots. During the winter the roots are growing as the limbs did during the spring and summer. The roots must grow to support the growth of the tree during the next spring and summer season.

Here is the amazing, wonderful and comforting truth: The peach tree during its winter season is just as much in the will and timing of God as it was during the spring and productive summer season. Thank God. After every winter season, spring comes again.

How do I know all of this to be true and real? Because I have gone through those seasons several times in my life and have counseled hundreds of saints, including ministers, who were going through their own winter seasons. If you have been a Christian for several years and are willing to be conformed to Christlikeness, then you have gone through a winter season and will go through a few more. All winters are not the same, for some are mild and some are very miserable. They do not last the same amount of time; some last for months and others a few weeks.

But those in the future will be different, for now you will know you are in a winter season, what it feels like and what it produces in you. You will know that all seasons are working together to produce more of the likeness of your Lord and Savior within you. You may not yet be fully able to do what Paul and Peter told us to do—to think it not strange concerning your fiery trial but to count it all joy, rejoice evermore and welcome the winter season as your friend. But at least you will have peace and know that you are still in the will and timing of God. You have not failed or made a mistake but are in God's Process for Conformity. This revelation will knock the "why me" out of your next winter season.

God's Tests Are Positive

My wife wrote another booklet called *God's Tests Are Positive*. She used the schoolroom to illustrate this truth. She also used several experiences that we went through to demonstrate it. I will share just one of her illustrations in this book to help you understand that God's tests are positive. God tests His children basically for the same reason a good teacher makes her students take tests.

The teacher does not have her students take tests because she is upset with them or wants to be mean to them. She tests them to see if they have learned what she has been teaching them. At the end of the school year, she gives major tests to see if the students are ready to graduate to a new level. In another area of this book, I will share a major test I went through that reveals this truth in a greater way.

The encouraging thing is that tests come only at the end of a learning process. If you arrive at question number nine in your test and you do not understand it or the principle necessary to solve the problem presented there, do not stay there. Skip it and go on and finish the test. You do not have to make one hundred percent to pass the test. Go ahead and hand your test in, and then you can go on summer vacation.

Some Christians never get beyond a certain place in their tests because they do not understand the principle of truth that will enable them to answer the "why" of the situation. Turn your test in to God and go home and get your textbook/ Bible and study the principle of the Law of Transformation and the Process for Conformity. Then when you think about the test, you will have revelation and peace in seeing how it all worked to produce more of the likeness of Christ within you. That is your joy, life and sense of fulfillment and satisfaction, so rejoice and be glad.

Tests Are Easier for the Prepared

Years ago, I was going through one of God's tests and was really struggling. I shared with my minister son, Tom, how I was having a hard time with what we were going through.

Tom said to me, "Dad, I have noticed when I take tests in school that if I have studied hard and really know the test material, I just whiz right through without any struggle. I hand my test to the teacher in a short time and leave the classroom feeling confident that I did well. But those who had not really learned what the teacher had taught or had not studied hard for the test struggled to the end of the class, and some were so discouraged that they did not turn their tests in." (By the way, Tom regularly made straight As on his report cards from kindergarten through college.)

I grasped the truth in his illustration and started seeking God to see what He had been teaching me during the last season. I also searched to see what I had been preaching that I was not practicing. I tell people jokingly that God will not even allow me to be an honest hypocrite; He makes me practice everything I preach. We are all in God's school, and our education will not stop until we obtain our doctoral degrees, which is conformity to the fullness of the maturity of Christ Jesus Himself.

The Scriptures declare that this schooling will continue

> till we all come to the unity of the faith and of the knowledge of the Son of God, to a perfect man [like the man Christ Jesus], to the measure of the stature of the fullness of Christ; that we . . . may grow up in all things into Him who is the head—Christ—from whom the whole body . . . does its share.
>
> Ephesians 4:13–16

We go "from glory to glory," from grade to grade, until we graduate into Christlikeness (2 Corinthians 3:18).

The Requirements of a Higher Calling

The principle of *the higher the calling, the greater the testing* is the reason I counsel young ministers not to pray and push for a higher calling unless they are willing to go through the greater testing, purifying and perfecting that it requires. This is the challenge Jesus gave two of His youngest disciples. James and John asked Jesus to give them the highest position, that of sitting on the right and left side of His throne.

Jesus did not rebuke them for making the request. He just asked them, "Are you able to drink from the cup that I

107

am about to drink from, and be baptized with the baptism I am baptized with?"

They replied enthusiastically, "We are able!"

Jesus told them they did not know what they were asking. They were probably thinking He was talking about the cup of Communion and His baptism in water. They had no idea that they were saying they could take the cup of rejection and persecution and the baptism of suffering.

Jesus said to them, "You will indeed drink My cup that I drink and be baptized with the baptism that I am baptized with. But I cannot grant your request now for the choice is not Mine to make, for it is for those for whom it is prepared by My Father."

They may have gone away believing that Jesus had granted their request if they met the conditions.

Being Tested through Pastoring

The president of the Bible college I attended was a real visionary. He inflamed our young minds with the idea that we were to be world changers and do great things for the Kingdom of God. I left college with the goal of demonstrating the Kingdom of God until we changed the world and brought King Jesus back. I wanted to be Oral Roberts, Billy Graham and T. L. Osborn all put together in one Bill Hamon.

God knew I was not ready and properly prepared to accomplish those things. Instead of fulfilling my zealous ambitions, He placed me in a pastoral position with a small congregation in a big old building. The church had gone through two years of continuous revival meetings from 1949 till 1951, but the pastor died of cancer and the church started falling apart. By the time I arrived in February 1954, the church had gone through several splits. Many temporary pastors had preached their own versions of the many doctrinal differences among the Pentecostals, such as the Godhead doctrines of Trinity and oneness, and the baptismal formulas of Father, Son and Holy Ghost or using Jesus' name only.

There were about 25 people left. I and a fellow student who came out of Bible College with me conducted a seven-week revival in that church in the little town of Toppenish, Washington. We were each nineteen years old. At the end of the revival my friend Keith went on to preach elsewhere. The elders there had asked me to stay on as pastor. I ended up staying for six years, got married and became the father of three children during that time.

But within one year of my arrival I was praying desperately, "Lord, have Your way, but what I am wanting is for You to get me out of here!" I felt I was dying there just pastoring those few people. I should be traveling in ministry preaching, prophesying and changing the world.

It was not until I died enough to self and my will that I could say, "Okay, God, if You want me to stay pastoring this church in this small town of five thousand people and never travel preaching beyond the state of Washington, I surrender to Your will."

That was my first major experience of God's process of death and transformation. It was the first major piece of the jigsaw puzzle of conformity to Christ's likeness and maturity. There would be many more pieces added over the rest of my life on earth before the picture was completed. Six months after I made that commitment, God released me to turn the church over to a young couple, and I started traveling in ministry. That was the first major step in God's fulfilling His predestined purpose for Bill Hamon's life and ministry. Romans 8:29.

My "Employees" Working for Me

There is a Scripture that God illuminated for me that has helped me have an overcoming attitude while going through God's Process for Conformity. That Scripture is 2 Corinthians 4:17: "For our light affliction, which is but for a moment, is working for us a far more exceeding and eternal weight of glory."

I could preach an hour on each phrase in this verse, but the one that the Holy Spirit impressed upon me with a personal application was *is working for us*. I looked at the Scripture again to see *what* is working for us. It is our light affliction. In other words, all my afflictions are working for me. They are my *employees*. Their work is producing *more of the fruit of the Spirit and the characteristics of Christ in my life*—love of my enemies, goodness, faith, forgiveness and especially long-suffering. I also gain wisdom going through the process and grace to be able to bless those who curse me and despitefully use me. The more they "afflict" me, the more of God's glory/Christlikeness is worked into my life. It is like what was said of the children of Israel in Egypt: "The more [the Egyptians] afflicted them, the more they multiplied and grew" (Exodus 1:12).

Second Corinthians 4:16 says, "Though our outward man is perishing, yet the inward man is being renewed day by day." Our natural, mortal man may be going through hell, but the inward, eternal, heavenly man is going from glory to glory until my *self* is conformed to the character and nature of Christ. "We who live are always delivered to death for Jesus' sake, that the life of Jesus also may be manifested in our mortal flesh" (2 Corinthians 4:11).

I tell you, saint, you need to know that God is out to kill your self-life so that Christ can live His life in you. When we finally take up our crosses of self-denial and let the life of Christ be our greatest joy, then we can live in peace and harmony with God. Romans 6:11 says, "Reckon yourselves to be dead indeed to sin, but alive to God in Christ Jesus our Lord."

Jesus declared, "If anyone desires to come after Me, let him deny himself, and take up his cross daily, and follow Me. For whoever desires to save his life will lost it, but whoever loses his life for My sake will save it" (Luke 9:23–24). *The Message* amplifies it some:

> Anyone who intends to come with me has to let me lead. You're not in the driver's seat—I am. Don't run from suffering; embrace it. Follow me and I'll show you how. Self-help is no help at all. Self-sacrifice is the way, my way, to finding yourself, your true self.

Paul wrote to the Galatian Christians that they were drifting away from the true Gospel and had lost what he had preached to them. He told them that they had lost God's main purpose of maturing them until they were conformed to the likeness of Christ. For that reason, he said, "I labor in birth . . . until Christ is formed in you" (Galatians 4:19). "For our light and momentary troubles are achieving for us an eternal glory [Christlikeness] that far outweighs them all" (2 Corinthians 4:17 NIV).

Our employees of tests, trials and troubles are achieving rewards for us that are eternal and will be a blessing throughout eternity. The blessings and eternal benefits are beyond our wildest dreams and imagination. Paul, who went through so much suffering, so many tests and trials, had a revelation of this reality of the Law of Transformation and the Process for Conformity that helped him to continue being an overcomer to the end of his life.

Paul knew it and declared it: "I have learned and practiced the key to successfully making it to the end: Keep your eyes on Jesus and the eternal reality." Jesus, for the joy that was set before Him, endured the cross. Jesus received the greatest reward and highest name because He paid the greatest price. The highest and greatest rewards are reserved for those who reach full maturity and become like Christ Jesus in all their thoughts, attitudes, decision-making, actions and way of life.

What Is Your Pleasure?

Have you ever taken pleasure in anything? If you were to name three things you take pleasure in what would they be? If you are a strong Christian, you might say worshiping God or reading God's Word. If, as a female, you think of natural things you might say shopping, family or joining friends for coffee. If you are a male, you might say playing or watching sports. If you are a loving family man, you might say your wife and kids.

I doubt, however, that any of us would choose what Paul put on his list of things he took pleasure in: "I take pleasure in *infirmities*, in *reproaches*, in *needs*, in *persecutions*, in *distresses*, for Christ's sake" (2 Corinthians 12:10, emphasis added). What could possibly motivate Paul to say he took pleasure in these depressing and negative experiences? Based on what Paul took pleasure in, a psychiatrist would have about five psychological terms to describe Paul's mental and emotional condition!

Either Paul was really weird in his thinking and attitude, or he had a revelation that was born of God within him. He must have received a revelation that gave him understanding of God's ways and purposes that is so much greater than what most modern-day saints have. Could Paul have received that insight when he was caught up to the third heaven and had his conversation with Jesus? Could it have something to do with the fact that his personal prophecy from Ananias included the words, "I will show Paul how many things he *must suffer* for My name's sake"? (See 2 Corinthians 12:2; Acts 9:16.)

Personally, I am glad that phrase has not been in any of the hundreds of personal prophecies I have received from others. Based on Paul's teaching, I believe Paul was saying this: "I take pleasure in all those things on my list because they are my employees working Christ's nature, character and all the essence of who Jesus is within me. Being like Jesus is my greatest passion, joy, purpose, pleasure and main motivation for continuing to keep living on earth. So why shouldn't I rejoice in those things that are working for me to produce my greatest desire and passion—to be like my Jesus?"

Paul expressed that in Philippians 3:10: "That I may know Him and the power of His resurrection, and the fellowship of His sufferings, being conformed to His death."

I Pay My "Employees"

If we really believe the Scriptures, we can declare that "if God is for us, who can be against us?" (Romans 8:31), that no person can put a curse on us if there is no unrighteousness within us and the shout of the King is in our midst (see Numbers 23:19–23), that no weapon formed against us shall prosper and every tongue that rises against us in judgment we shall condemn (see Isaiah 54:17), and that we are more than conquerors through Christ who loved us and gave His life for us (see Romans 8:37).

With that all being true we definitely should believe that these light afflictions are working for us. Since, therefore, they are working for you and me, then we are their employers and should pay our employees.

If people begin to afflict me with words of ridicule, accusation, belittling or any other type of verbal affliction, I take my billfold out of my pocket, take some money out and offer it to them.

They ask, "What is that for?"

I tell them, "I pay my employees."

They may say, "I'm not your employee."

I respond, "Yes, you really are, because the Bible says that words of criticism and abuse given to afflict me are working for me. They are working into me some of the nature of my Lord Jesus. And you are working long-suffering, mercy, endurance, grace and forgiveness within me. So let me pay you for the very effective work you are doing for me."

Sometimes when I am preaching this truth and using this example, I will pick out a couple in the front row and give a twenty-dollar bill to the wife, saying, "When your husband starts giving you a bad time just give him this money."

She will sometimes give it to him right away, and he will start to give it back to me.

I say, "No, no, you keep it, for you will probably be giving it to her next week." Of course, this is done in a friendly manner with smiles and a pleasant attitude.

If you did this same thing, the transaction would be doing more for you than for the one you offer the money to, because it keeps you from getting upset or angry or getting your feelings hurt. It reminds you not to be offended, for that person is doing you more good than damage. You are reacting to it with the right spirit and attitude.

Now you can see why I say that all I have are friends and employees! Not only do all my afflicting situations work for me, but all things are working together for my good to make me successful in my predestined highest calling. The illustration does help get the point across.

We will now continue by using illustrations that show how the Process for Conformity really works. I will then describe a three-week period that my wife and I went through that was the most challenging and transforming we ever experienced. You will be blessed by the revelation and transforming truths that Jesus revealed after the Process for Conformity was over.

ACKNOWLEDGMENT & PETITION

Lord, I now see that when You are for me, then no one can effectively be against me. For You make my tests, trials and afflictions my friends and employees. They are made to work for me, helping me to be conformed to Your likeness. I have the revelation and understanding; now give me Your more abundant, supernatural, divine, enabling grace so that I can "count it all joy," "rejoice evermore" and "in all things give thanks"—continually keeping faith and a positive mental attitude. As You did with the apostle Paul, teach me how and enable me to "take pleasure" in the workings of the Process for Conformity to the likeness of Christ Jesus. Like Jesus, I will make it through victoriously by seeing the joy that is set before me for being an overcomer. I will make it by His grace.

7

Major Examples of the Conforming Process

Therefore we do not lose heart. Even though our outward man is perishing, yet the inward man is being renewed day by day. For our light affliction, which is but for a moment, is working for us a far more exceeding and eternal weight of glory.

2 Corinthians 4:16–17

We want our transitory lives to be absorbed into the life that is eternal. If Christians only think of the present, temporary world conditions, they will become discouraged and dismayed. If we think more of the eternal and heavenly rewards, we will not become discouraged. Look at the above verses and then see how the Phillips paraphrase presents this same truth but with different wording:

This is the reason why we never collapse. The outward man does indeed suffer wear and tear, but every day the inward man receives fresh strength. These little troubles (which are really so transitory) are winning for us a permanent, glorious and solid reward out of all proportion to our pain. For we are looking all the time not at the visible things but at the invisible. The visible things are transitory: it is the invisible things that are really permanent.

2 Corinthians 4:16–18

Paul declared that there are three main enabling forces that empower us to be overcomers—faith, hope and love (see 1 Corinthians 13:13). Faith keeps and helps us in the present, but hope enables us to face the present problems by looking to the glorious future God has planned for us on this earth and for eternity. Love will help us with our problems in our relationships with all the different kinds of people we have to deal with. These three forces will also enable us to go through the conforming Process God plans to use to make us in the likeness of Jesus Christ.

The Illuminating Illustration: The Human Hand

The Lord gave me an illustration that helps us understand how Romans 8:28 works together with Romans 8:29. It also makes it clearer how the Law of Transformation and the Process for Conformity work for God to fulfill His highest calling for man.

The *human hand* is used for this illustration. The *four fingers* represent the *outward man* of our being. They represent every area of the natural life—financial, social, physical,

The laws of natural man, represented by the fingers, are not lessened but superseded by a higher purpose of God, represented by the thumb.

inner eternal self

outer natural self

marital, family, health, possessions, in fact everything we are, do and go through on this earth. The outward man includes our mortal physical bodies; the soul is also included because it comprises the mind, emotions and will; it is a part of the temporary being of man that is included in the Transformation and the Process.

The eternal spirit of man, which is the *inner man*, is represented by the *thumb*. The inner man speaks of our inner and eternal being. It is the part of our being that Jesus is transforming into His likeness. The soul is also included because it is part of one's eternal being. The soul is the body of the spirit just as the physical body is the body of the soul. The soul functions between the body and the spirit of man. The soul is what we call our "self." The soul-self is neutral. It functions based on influence either by the physical natural man, which is carnal influence, or by the inner man, which is our born-again spirit having the Spirit of God.

When the Bible speaks of flesh and spirit it is talking about these two entities of our being. The term *flesh* means the carnal self-life. That is the reason Paul declares that those

119

who are living in the flesh cannot please God; if you live according to the flesh you shall die, but if you put to death the deeds of the body you shall live. Romans 8:1–13 and Galatians 5:16–26 both give contrasting lists of the works of the flesh and the life-fruit of the Spirit. The soul contains the imagination, but again, it is greatly influenced by the spirit and the body.

When a Christian dies, the physical body goes to the grave, awaiting the day of the resurrection of the righteous. That is when this body of dust will be redeemed and transformed into an immortal, glorified eternal body. Then that body will be joined with the spirit body, which has been functioning in heaven ever since they were separated. Then the Christian will be a whole human being—spirit, soul and body, one entity that shall function forever as an eternal spirit, soul and body being.

Beginning to Understand Why

As you read this text, remember the illustration. The *four fingers* of the hand represent *our outward natural life*. The *thumb* represents *our inner spirit life*.

God will allow our natural lives to go through biblical experiences such as Job endured in order to develop more of the *nature* and character of Jesus in our inner man, transforming the soul-life from a humanistic self-life to the Christ-life. In my 66 years of ministry, after evaluating the trials and tests that I have gone through, studying the biblical heroes of the faith and counseling thousands of saints, I have discovered that everyone who is predestined to be conformed to the likeness of Jesus Christ, and especially those called to greater leadership, will go through several traumatic experiences in their lifetimes. I call those experiences heartbreaking, mind-blowing, hopeless-feeling, world-shaking situations. Things that you would think a Christian should never have to suffer.

It makes the mind want to cry out, *How could this happen to us, Lord? We have lived for You faithfully. We have done everything we know to be pleasing to You! We prayed and committed everything to You, and still this horrible thing happened. Lord, I can't take one thing more! Why me, Lord?* You may even feel as Jesus did on the cross—"My God, My God, why have You forsaken Me?"

I am sure that when Jesus was resurrected to heaven, Father God explained to His Son that He had not forsaken Him, and all that He suffered worked together for His good to fulfill His predestined purpose for coming to earth—to suffer, bleed and die on the cross to redeem man and portray to all eternal creation God's core nature of love. If we still have need of answers when we get to heaven, Jesus will explain the "why" of it all. In the meantime, we will live victoriously by the revelation of the Law of Transformation and the Process for Conformity. Let me share one of these experiences that my wife and I suffered through.

The Background of Our Conforming Process

My wife and I had a three-week, major Process for Conformity experience in June 1981. A little background to that time period. In 1978 I started writing my first book, *The Eternal Church*. It took three years to finish. All 395 pages were written by hand and then typed on my manual portable typewriter. When it reached final manuscript stage, I bought one of the new electric typewriters for my secretary to finalize the manuscript for printing.

The year before, we had moved CI headquarters from San Antonio, Texas, to Phoenix, Arizona. We caravanned ten families and all of CI's college material for the thousand miles to northern Phoenix. Johnny Cash had earned his associate degree at CI's college extension in Nashville, Tennessee. In May 1978 I presented Johnny's degree to him at his House of Cash, which was his recording studio and headquarters. The event was televised when I was interviewed by the Christian Broadcasting Network three weeks later. Johnny asked me to come back later and perform the wedding ceremony for one of his daughters. A few weeks later, June Carter Cash received an honorary doctorate from a university in California. They were having a great celebration and wanted me to be one of the three speakers, which included Larry Gatlin and the mayor of Nashville.

During this time, in March 1979, we started the Friday night School of the Holy Spirit. Our son Timothy married Karen Pewton on April 13 of that year. Our daughter, Sherilyn, married Pastor Glenn Miller on August 15, 1980. Tom had attended Christ For The Nations Institute. He met Jane there, and they scheduled their wedding to take place on June 13, 1981, in Little Rock, Arkansas, where Jane's family lived.

In the meantime, Evelyn's dad, who was living with us, died in May 1979 at age 67. Evelyn's younger sister and her husband, Donna and Leon Walters, and their three daughters closed down their business in Denver, moved to Phoenix and lived in our house with us until we all moved to Florida five years later. We also bought and lost property during that time, which was one of my other conforming processes that I will share about in another place in this book.

When I was writing *The Eternal Church*, it kept taking longer and longer than I had anticipated. I had promised my wife that we would go to Hawaii for two weeks for our 25th wedding anniversary, which was August 13, 1980. We celebrated our 25th anniversary, but no trip to Hawaii. I then promised my wife that I would take her when the book was finished and in the hands of the publisher. That happened in May 1981, and we went on vacation.

The Three-Week Major Process Begins

We have progressed now to that three-week time period. Evelyn and I began to make preparations to drive to Tom and Jane's June wedding. A number of us were traveling together in a van and a seventeen-foot cab-overhang motor home. We all drove from Phoenix to Oklahoma City and arrived there the next morning. We filled up with gas, had breakfast and prayed for a continued safe journey.

Evelyn and I climbed into the van with the couple who would be doing the wedding music. In the motor home was a total of nine family members: Leon and Donna Walters and their three girls; Evelyn's other sister, Marilyn, and her two daughters, Tonya, age nine, and Crystal, age six; and Evelyn's mother.

The motor home took off first, and we followed but could not get on the freeway as soon as they did. As we drove about a mile down the freeway, we noticed that all the vehicles ahead of us were slowing down quite quickly. As I looked ahead, I saw a vehicle upside down on the highway and bursting into flames.

I realized it was our motor home.

I was not driving, so I opened the door and hit the ground running before the van fully stopped. When I arrived, I saw that Leon had gotten most of them out. Evelyn's mom was lying with her legs still caught in the wreckage. The motor home had skidded 187 feet upside down on the highway, and the gas tanks were shooting up flames. All my mother-in-law's clothes were ripped off except her panties and bra. I grabbed her under the arms to pull her out of the wreck, but her legs were entangled in the metal.

I realized that jerking her out was apt to break her legs, but just then the wind pushed the flames over her. I had the desperate choice to either rip her out and possibly break her legs or hesitate knowing they would burn badly. I pulled and her legs came free without breaking. I laid her on the side of the road and rushed around to see if I could reach someone else.

Then I saw Crystal, my little six-year-old niece. The lower half of her body was extending out from under the wreck. I grabbed ahold of her legs to try to pull her out, but her body was pressed to the ground. I knew that if I pulled hard enough I might come out with half a body, but in the next second the wind changed and blew twenty-foot flames straight toward me knocking me backward. Leon had just pulled his oldest daughter out from where she had been stuck hanging halfway out, and he was able to free her without tearing or breaking any part of her body.

Marilyn, Crystal's mother, was screaming, "My daughter is in these flames! Somebody do something!"

Evelyn was crying and wailing, "God, where are You?" Eight members of her family were hurt, and her niece was being consumed in the flames.

Our hearts were stunned at having to leave the child, but we were forced to back off because of the fierceness of the flames. All the people who had gotten out of their cars to watch were moving away and yelling that it was going to blow.

Emergency vehicles began to arrive. Ambulances took some of the injured to one hospital and others to another. Evelyn and I stayed until the fire burned down; all the tires, which were sticking up in the air, were burned off the rims. We waited until the wrecker came, for Crystal was still under the tangled, burned metal. When the wrecker lifted the body of the motor home, we saw Crystal lying between the upper and lower insulation in the over cab where she had been riding. Though her lower body was burned to a crisp, her upper body was preserved; even her long blond hair was not burned. When we had the funeral, we were able to have an open casket.

We visited everyone in the hospital. Evelyn's mom was badly hurt and was in a life-and-death struggle. Leon and Donna and the two older girls were bruised but not seriously damaged. Devra, their youngest daughter, was extremely skinned all over. Marilyn and her older daughter had no serious damage, but Crystal was taken to the morgue.

Transition to the Wedding

Evelyn had to buy under- and outer clothes for all the females, because their luggage and purses were all burned in the wreck. After we made sure everyone had clothing and some money to survive a few days, we took Leon and

Donna's two oldest daughters, Dee and Donnetta, with us, for they were scheduled to be in Tom and Jane's wedding.

We left late that afternoon and drove the 330 miles to Little Rock. The next night we had the wedding rehearsal and the next day, the wedding. It was a beautiful wedding; everything went smoothly. Amazingly, everyone did well. I performed the ceremony. My mom and dad and older brother and his wife were there. That was the only wedding that any of my family had the opportunity to attend, including Evelyn's and mine and our other two children's.

Progressing to the Funeral

After the wedding our hearts were wrenched again as we all drove the five hundred miles to Orange, Texas, to have the funeral for Crystal at a little town outside of Orange called Hartsburg, where Marilyn's father-in-law owned a graveyard. I preached at the sad funeral, and then Evelyn and I said our farewells to the rest of the families and started driving the four-hundred-plus miles to conduct a preaching and prophesying conference at Ken Sumrall's church and Bible college in Pensacola, Florida.

The hotel that was booked for us gave us an experience we have never had in any other hotel. When we looked out the window the next morning we saw a graveyard full of big tombstones within thirty feet of our window. It shook my wife terribly, for we had just come from Crystal's funeral.

I preached five times and prophesied to about 250 people. At the close of the meeting, we drove seventy miles to De-Funiak Springs, Florida, where our daughter and son-in-law were pastoring.

"I Cannot Take One Thing More!"

While we were driving to their place Evelyn said, "I feel as though every nerve in my body is on fire. I can't take one thing more."

Sherilyn and Glenn had some horses at their place. When we arrived, Glenn and I decided to go horseback riding, hoping it would be relaxing and take some pressure off. We saw a dune buggy in the barn where the horses were stabled, and after riding a bit decided to go back and take that around for a while.

Evelyn said to Glenn, "Do not let my husband get hurt, for I cannot take one thing more."

While driving the dune buggy, I turned too fast and tilted it over. I broke both bones in my left forearm.

Glenn called Evelyn and told her and Sherilyn to get ready, for they all needed to rush me to the hospital in Fort Walton.

She yelled at Glenn, "Don't joke with me!"

He said, "I wish I were joking, but it's true."

It took them awhile to get me into the operating room, and after a couple of hours Evelyn asked Glenn to go and see if he could find out what was happening.

Sherilyn had gone to get everyone something to eat, and while Evelyn was sitting there alone God spoke to her: *Evelyn, do you remember what you said when you were driving here from Pensacola?*

"Lord," she replied, "I said a lot of things. Which one are You asking about?"

Didn't you say you could not take one more thing?

"Yes, I did—and I meant it! I can't take one more tragedy in my life!"

Is your husband's broken arm one more tragedy?

"Yes, Lord, it is!"

You said you couldn't take one thing more, so what are you going to do about it?

She thought about this. *I could go out and get drunk*, she reasoned, *but I wouldn't know what to buy to get drunk.* (Evelyn was saved when she was three and filled with the Spirit when she was seven, and she had very little inclination to being worldly.) She thought she could have a nervous breakdown, but that sounded like an impractical thing to do.

She thought a little more and then said to God, "I don't know what I can do but stay trusting and living for You."

Then God said something to her that surprised and shocked her. *Evelyn*, He said, *I love you, but don't you ever threaten Me like that again! I alone know how much you can take, and I promised you I would never allow you to go through something that I knew you couldn't handle.*

That was not what she expected God to say to her. She thought God could have shown a little concern and compassion after what she had just gone through. Nevertheless, it did something within that made her never again worry about what the future might hold for her.

The doctor still did not want to release me after five days, but I checked myself out of the hospital with my arm in a cast, and we flew to Oklahoma to attend my mom and dad's fiftieth wedding anniversary celebration.

God's Purpose for the Process

That finished our three weeks of intense training in the Law of Transformation and the Process for Conformity. Those principles were working to conform us to Christ Jesus. They were also helping determine if we could pass the tests that would prove whether or not we were ready for the next phase of God's purpose to be fulfilled in and through us. This process was one of the most traumatic tests we have ever gone through. During the time of the accident was the first time I ever heard my wife question God with a "why" and feel as though God had forsaken us. We had prayed and pleaded the blood of Jesus to cover us and for the angels to watch over us, but this still happened.

Why?

I must admit that I struggled much with what had happened until God explained why. There was a purpose in it all, but I did not understand until God used a natural illustration that made sense out of the senselessness. He used something that I was somewhat familiar with.

For three weeks before my wife and I got married, I worked helping to lay a railroad track. We laid the crossties and then nailed the steel rails to them. We also used big screws to drill down into the wood crossties.

God said He was testing me in this three-week process to see if I was qualified and ready to enter into the new ministry He had planned for me to fulfill. He was processing me just as manufacturers process the steel rails before they are placed on the crossties. In the bigger picture of great railroad tracks, there are engines that pull railroad cars loaded with cargo worth millions of dollars. Then there are passenger trains that convey numerous people—all on those steel rails.

God said that the revelation and ministry He wanted to give me would be like those steel rails. Thousands of lives and all kinds of cargo depend on steel-rail tracks to be of a quality that can endure constant pressure over the years and faithfully maintain their integrity so all those passengers and workers can travel with confidence.

Steel Rails: Forging Quality and Dependability

The way steel rails are made is very interesting and challenging, especially when your life is compared to the process. It begins with raw steel being heated enough to melt it down into a liquid and poured into a form in the shape that the rails are supposed to be.

The rails are then put through the process. Each rail is placed in the hottest condition it could ever be in. It is then put through twisting, pulling and all kinds of stress and pressure. The steel rail is allowed to come back to normal temperature. If it has not cracked or become misshapen but retains its straight shape, then it is considered for use on the track.

But it has one more test. It is then placed in the coldest condition it could ever be in. It goes through the same testing as it did in the hot test. When it is warmed back to normal temperature, if it has no cracks, warps or imperfections that could hinder its trustworthiness and integrity to make it through any extreme weather that earth could put it through, it is put on the track for years of dependable service.

We Went through the Steel-Rail Test

God took us through the test of the hottest and then the coldest. It was like a roller coaster doing loops, round and round, one after the other. The top of the loop typifies the hot part of the test. The bottom of the loop represents the cold part of the test.

 Hot! Evelyn and I enjoyed our two-week vacation, came home and made joyful preparations to go to our son's wedding. Hot: top of the loop.

 Cold! We traveled all night with our family and had a wonderful breakfast. We prayed before getting on the freeway but, suddenly, a wreck. Our family faced the devastation of death, injuries, hospital stays—even the disruptive loss of material things like suitcases and purses with licenses and credit cards. We sadly had to leave family members behind. Cold: bottom of the loop.

 Hot! In the midst of our pain, we had a wonderful wedding and received into the family a tremendous daughter-in-law, Jane Makosky, now Jane Hamon. We had good fellowship with friends and family. Hot: top of the loop again.

 Cold! We had to face the raw emotion of the funeral of our little niece. Our family was awash in sadness and heartbreaking tears. Cold: bottom of the loop again.

 Hot! We needed to drive immediately to conference meetings, where I preached five times and prophesied to 250 people. The people at the meetings were all happy and rejoicing. Hot: top of the loop again.

 Cold! We drove to our daughter's place where I broke my arm and wound up in the hospital for five days.

Evelyn can't handle one thing more. Cold: bottom of
the loop again.

 Hot! Evelyn and I drove to Oklahoma for my parents'
fiftieth wedding anniversary. It was a special, happy
time with family and friends. Hot: back to the top of
loop.

Back to Normal! We then drove home and leveled out
to the normal, challenging and enjoyable life of family and ministry.

Evelyn and I must have passed the test, for two years later
Jesus gave me the revelation of the "Company of Prophets"
that God is raising up in these last days. He revealed to me
that the prophets were to be restored fully to a recognized and
active role in the Church. They were to prepare the way and
make ready a people for the coming of the Lord as prophesied by Isaiah, Malachi and Zacharias, the father of John the
Baptist. I wrote the book *Prophets and Personal Prophecy* to
bring the revelation to the Church. At that time 99 percent of
the Church did not believe that prophets were to exist in the
Church in the twentieth century. Now, after pioneering the
restoration of prophets for over three decades, I can confirm
that prophets are accepted in a large portion of the Body of
Christ, and there are thousands of prophets around the world.

Why Transformation and Conformity to Christ?

God had an eternal plan for us to fulfill when He created humanity. Jesus birthed and is building His Church to fulfill an

eternal purpose, which is "according to the eternal purpose which He accomplished in Christ Jesus our Lord" (Ephesians 3:11).

God needs a certain number of individuals who have come to the fullness of all that Christ is in their thinking, attitudes, convictions, beliefs—in fact, all that Jesus is in all areas. Father God has already appointed His resurrected Son to rule and reign over all that He oversees. Father God has made Jesus heir of everything God is and has. "In these last days [Father God has] spoken to us by His Son, whom He has appointed heir of all things" (Hebrews 1:2). God has been looking for and choosing those who qualify to be joint heirs, who will co-labor with His Son over all that He shall inherit.

A percentage of those have already been chosen from the Old Testament saints, but the majority will be chosen from the saints in the Church. God wants children He can trust to execute His affairs as much as He trusts His only begotten Son, Jesus Christ. Jesus proved His trustworthiness and absolute submission to the will and purposes of Father God during His time as a mortal man on earth. We are in the process of being tested, tried and proven by God's Process for Conformity to determine who will pass the tests and qualify to be chosen by Christ to co-reign with Him.

God has been using His Law of Transformation and His Process for Conformity since He began with Adam and Eve in the Garden. He has continued the process down through the ages. I would imagine that He is getting close to the total number He planned to receive from His humankind creation.

Only Overcomers Will Rule with Christ

All that it takes to be qualified for heaven is to be born again by having the blood of Jesus wash away all your sins and to be in right relationship with God when you come to the pearly gates of entry into heaven. Everyone who makes it into heaven will have his or her own special place to dwell and will have special service to King Jesus for joy and fulfillment throughout eternity.

But the only ones whom God will place in major roles of rulership and responsibility are those who have been tested in all areas and have proven that they have died to their self-motivated life and have been transformed into being motivated by the Christ-life. They have demonstrated that their complete will is in submission to God the Father as Jesus' will was fully submitted during His time as mortal man on earth, especially during His greatest test and challenge in the Garden of Gethsemane. There is no "why" in their thinking or conversations about God's allowances. Through God's Process for Conformity they have been delivered from murmuring and complaining. Those chosen saints no longer question or doubt God. They *know* God and are His trustworthy friends. They have finally become conformed to the likeness of Christ and are one with Him in Spirit and in truth.

The other very important requirement for the chosen is this: They have faithfully fulfilled their ministry as members of the Body of Christ. God's eternal rewards for His people are not based on how great they were in man's eyes during their time on earth but on how much they were conformed to Christlikeness and faithfully fulfilled their God-given ministries.

Those are the two main things Jesus will use to determine His rewards for His children: "Well done, good/Christlike and faithful servant—you fulfilled your membership ministry." Those are the words we all want to hear when we stand alone before the Judge of all humankind. I am not ambitious for rewards of position in rulership with Christ, and neither do I have the attitude expressed in the old songs, "Lord, build me a cabin in the corner of Glory Land," or "Lord, if I can just make it in." Jesus gave His all for me, and I want to give my all for Him.

When I was in my twenties, as James and John were when they asked Jesus if they could be in the highest position with Him, I probably would have done the same. But now in my eighties after decades of ministry, I am just praying for the grace, wisdom and humble submission to make it through God's Process for Conformity to the full nature of Christ Jesus.

What Matters Most to God

God's highest calling, His top priority and purpose for man, is not great accomplishments in this world. God was in Christ reconciling the world unto Himself, not unto great ministry. As important as great accomplishments and successful ministry are, that should not be our number one goal in life. If we understand and are committed to God's greatest and foremost desire for His people, we will have a much more satisfied and fulfilled life and ministry, avoiding many discouragements.

God's first and foremost desire for His children is

not the apostle who has thousands of churches and a miraculous ministry,

not the prophet prophesying to the nations and thousands of people,

not the pastor of a congregation of tens of thousands of people with an international television ministry,

not the evangelist conducting crusades with hundreds of thousands attending and multitudes being saved,

not the teacher who has written numerous books and speaks in the most prestigious universities,

not the Christian businessman or woman with great wealth giving millions of dollars to the Church and charity, and

not the Christian who is president or leader of a nation.

Though all these things are needed in Christ's Church and are necessary for God's purpose for fulfilling all He wants from the human race, they are not His number one desire and purpose, and they do not qualify us for God's highest calling for His people.

First Corinthians 13:1–3 reveals *the reason why Christlikeness is the most important calling* and carries the highest priority with God.

Though I speak with the tongues of men and of angels, but have not love, I have become sounding brass or a clanging cymbal. And though I have the gift of prophecy, and understand all mysteries and all knowledge, and though I have all faith, so that I could remove mountains, but have not love, I am nothing. And though I bestow all my goods to feed the poor, and though I give my body to be burned, but have not love, it profits me nothing.

First John 4:16 declares that "God is love, and he who abides in love abides in God, and God in him." The Bible does not say that God *has* love, but that God *is* love. Divine love is God, and God is love! Whatever God is, Jesus is, so we can say that Jesus Christ is love. Since *love* is the same as *Christlikeness*, it would be the same to say that without Christlikeness motivating the outer works, they are nothing.

The Bible conveys that without love all our great accomplishments and mighty works amount to nothing in God's sight. If we became the greatest of the great in man's eyes, but we did not do it with the nature and character of Christ, and our motives were not to bring glory to God but to build our greatness, then all our works count for nothing.

The Message says it like this:

If I speak with human eloquence and angelic ecstasy but don't love, I'm nothing but the creaking of a rusty gate. If I speak God's Word with power, revealing all his mysteries and making everything plain as day, and if I have faith that says to a mountain, "Jump," and it jumps, but I don't love, I'm nothing. If I give everything I own to the poor and even go to the stake to be burned as a martyr, but I don't love, I've gotten nowhere. So, no matter what I say, what I believe, and what I do, I'm bankrupt without love. . . . But for right now, until that completeness, we have three things to do to lead us toward that consummation: Trust steadily in God, hope unswervingly, love extravagantly. And the best of the three is love.

1 Corinthians 13:1–3, 13

Any way we look at it, the Scriptures declare that love (Christlikeness) is the most important thing to possess, must be the most prominent thing in our ministries and must be our number one priority in life. Without Christlikeness, the motivation for everything we do does not count for much in God's estimation. We hope that the "profits nothing" does not include entrance into heaven.

We do not know the fullness of what Paul and the Holy Spirit meant by "it profits me nothing." The ministries and works he described cover the teaching and work of most of the ministries within Christendom. Nothing is zero; not one thing. We know we are saved by grace and faith in the Lord Jesus Christ; still we hope that salvation is not included in the "nothing."

Jesus tells us in Matthew 7:21–23 that many will say on that final day statements like, "Lord, we preached and prophesied in Your name; we even cast out devils and had signs and wonders in our ministries. And, in addition, we did a lot of humanitarian works."

But He will have to reply to many of them, "Depart from me, you workers of lawlessness. I don't accept you, and you cannot enter heaven."

Basically, they did the works of Christ, but they did not live the life of Christ. Nor had they allowed God to conform them to Christlikeness. They had the outward man manifesting but not the inward man possessing the character and nature of Jesus Christ. Paul declared that the only faith-works that count with God are the ones done by "faith working through love" (Galatians 5:6).

Could It Happen to Me?

I wrote a book called *How Can These Things Be?*, which covers this subject thoroughly. The subtitle reads: *A Preacher and a Miracle Worker but Denied Heaven!*

Wow! How can these things be?

The prophet Balaam had a true prophetic ministry; in fact, he gave the only Messianic prophecy in the book of Numbers. There is no way anyone could call him a false prophet by his ministry, for he gave true prophecies and they came to pass. The Bible indicates that this is the main way to judge a prophet: His prophecies come to pass (see Deuteronomy 18:22).

That tells you whether or not the prophecy was true, but it does not reveal the inward character of the prophet. In other words, you judge prophets and prophecy differently. You judge prophecy on its content and the prophet on his or her character. Preachers do not always practice what they preach and prophesy, and Christians do not always walk their talk or possess what they profess. Many modern-day preachers would have a present-day Balaam prophet on their television shows because of his reputation: Whatever he prophesies comes to pass; whoever he blesses is blessed, and whoever he curses is cursed. That was why King Balak was willing to pay Balaam a tremendous amount of money to come and prophesy curses over Israel.

There is very little evidence to call Balaam a false prophet from the record of his works, but Jesus, Peter and Jude referred to him as a false prophet. This is because his outward ministry was right, but his inward motivation and character were wrong.

If you think you might be in this category of individuals, or if you are not sure, 1 Corinthians 3:13–15 AMPC may give you hope.

> The work of each [one] will become [plainly, openly] known (shown for what it is); for the day [of Christ] will disclose and declare it, because it will be revealed with fire, and the fire will test and critically appraise the character and worth of the work each person has done. If the work which any person has built on this Foundation [any product of his efforts whatever] survives [this test], he will get his reward. But if any person's work is burned up [under the test], he will suffer the loss [of it all, losing his reward], though he himself will be saved, but only as [one who has passed] through fire.

Let me encourage you not to take a chance on being saved by going through the fire. Please give God permission—show your desire and willingness—to go through the Process for Conformity. Pay close attention to how plain and straightforward *The Message* makes this subject. These are the direct teachings of Jesus as He was instructing His disciples with the crowds listening.

> "Don't look for shortcuts to God. The market is flooded with surefire, easygoing formulas for a successful life that can be practiced in your spare time. Don't fall for that stuff, even though crowds of people do. The way to life—to God!—is vigorous and requires total attention.

"Be wary of false preachers who smile a lot, dripping with practiced sincerity. Chances are they are out to rip you off some way or other. Don't be impressed with charisma; look for character. Who preachers *are* is the main thing, not what they say. A genuine leader will never exploit your emotions or your pocketbook. These diseased trees with their bad apples are going to be chopped down and burned.

"Knowing the correct password—saying 'Master, Master,' for instance—isn't going to get you anywhere with me. What is required is serious obedience—*doing* what my Father wills. I can see it now—at the Final Judgment thousands strutting up to me and saying, 'Master, we preached the Message, we bashed the demons, our God-sponsored projects had everyone talking.' And do you know what I am going to say? 'You missed the boat. All you did was use me to make yourselves important. You don't impress me one bit. You're out of here.'

"These words I speak to you are not incidental additions to your life, homeowner improvements to your standard of living. They are foundational words, words to build a life on."

Matthew 7:13–24

How Prophecies and Dreams Test the Saints

In 1953 I drove my 1948 Studebaker sixteen hundred miles from Amarillo, Texas, to Portland, Oregon, to attend Bible college. The church I attended in Oregon was a newly formed, independent Latter Rain church seeking to incorporate the truths and ministries of the Latter Rain movement. Most of the saints came from holiness and Pentecostal churches that had very strong preaching against worldliness. It was mainly directed to the women to wear long dresses, long hair, no makeup and no earrings. All amusements and sports were counted worldly, the worst being going to a movie theater. I had attended Assemblies of God churches, which had most of those antiworldly standards, before I started attending this church.

When I returned for a visit the following summer, I was shocked at what I saw. The church had completely changed. The women had embraced the present fashion of the world— short hair, all kinds of cosmetics and earrings, and short, tight dresses with four-inch spiked heels.

Now, you might think, *What's wrong with that? Women freely dress that way today.*

Yes, the females in my family and church dress that way as well. But this church went from one extreme to another. They set up a liquor bar in the basement where they offered alcoholic drinks and worldly music and dancing. This was several years before "praise dancing" was allowed in any churches. The pastor and some of the men started smoking cigars and drinking beer. I was astounded by the change.

What had happened? A preacher had come to the church and preached "greasy-grace": It is called "hyper-grace" in this 21st century. The essence of the teaching was that we live in the spirit, so all that counts is that your spirit is right. What you do in the flesh does not matter, for you are a spirit being. The grace of God gives you the freedom to do anything you want to do with your natural being. You are no longer under the law of right and wrong. There is no wrong for God's people, for to the pure all things are pure.

Needless to say, I was very confused about the whole matter. It was discovered that the pastor was in an adulterous relationship with the worship leader, a younger woman, but nothing was done about it. The wife of an elder in the church said, "I always thought Christians should be able to have all the pleasures of this life and still be good Christians."

I cried out to God and asked Him what was going on here. Why had such an extreme position been embraced? How could this have happened to this church?

He said, *Your answer is in Deuteronomy 13:1–4.*

I had no idea what those verses were about, so I turned to them and read:

> "If there arises among you a prophet or a dreamer of dreams, and he gives you a sign or a wonder, and the sign or the wonder comes to pass, of which he spoke to you, saying, 'Let us go after other gods'—which you have not known— 'and let us serve them,' you shall not listen to the words of that prophet or that dreamer of dreams, for the LORD your God is testing you to know whether you love the LORD your God with all your heart and with all your soul. You shall walk after the LORD your God and fear Him, and keep His commandments and obey His voice; you shall serve Him and hold fast to Him."

Tests Prove What We Really Believe

God was declaring that He allowed that preacher to present his extreme teaching to the people to see if the holiness and righteousness born of God was really in them or if they were just following something someone had taught. Were they secretly looking for justification to do whatever pleased them?

Why did it happen? Because the Lord your God is *testing* you.

For what purpose is the *testing*? To know whether or not you *love* the Lord your God with all your *heart* and with all your *soul*. God told His people that they had to keep His commandments and obey the *voice* of the Lord.

Remember Jesus' first Commandment—the one that is the most important to Him: You shall love the Lord your God with all your heart, soul, mind and strength (see Mark 12:30). If you do not know God's commandments and His voice, you are in danger of being talked into something that is not according to the Word of God. That is the reason the Bible authors exhort us to study God's Word, memorize it and know it to the extent we can recognize false teaching. We also need to have our spiritual senses exercised enough to recognize whether a prophecy is the voice of the Lord or just the thought of an individual. He calls us to be among "those who by reason of use have their senses exercised to discern both good and evil" (Hebrews 5:14).

Truth from Thumb and Fingers Illustration

Consider again the thumb and fingers illustration.

> The *hand* represents the whole being of man.
> The *four fingers* illustrate every area of our natural lives.
> The *thumb* illustrates our inner spiritual-eternal man.

God is concerned with our whole being—body, soul and spirit; both the outward man and the inner man. The body of the natural man is temporary; however, the inner man is eternal. That is one reason God puts the most importance and priority on the inner man. He makes the natural part of man subject to God's higher purposes and processes for perfecting the inner man. They are for conforming the eternal man into the likeness of Jesus Christ. He will make the natural outward man's body like His glorious body at the first resurrection.

God's Will Is for Our Best

It is essential that we establish the fact that God's Word reveals, in both the Old and New Testaments, that it is God's will and desire for all aspects of our natural lives to be healthy and prosperous. Jesus was wounded for our transgressions, bruised for our iniquities. The chastisement for our peace was upon Jesus, and by His stripes we are healed.

Deuteronomy 28:1–14 declares that if we hear and obey the voice of the Lord and keep His commandments, then everything we have and do will be blessed. Our families will be blessed; our businesses will prosper; we will be successful socially and financially. We will loan and not borrow; we will be the head and not the tail; we will be above and not beneath. We will be victorious every day in every way. We will have the golden touch, which causes everything we get involved with to prosper. Even our enemies will be at peace with us. God will be for us, and nobody can be against us. The Bible portrays that all this is God's will, pleasure and purpose for His children.

Herein lies the dilemma and confusing part for a Christian.

How can our trials, tests and sufferings be in the will of God when they negatively affect these blessed areas of our lives?

There is an answer! Yes, all those blessings in our lives are God's desire and will for us, but there is a higher desire, will and purpose of God that supersedes all other desires of God. There are God's laws of prosperity, healing, etc., but there is a higher Law of Transformation and Process for Conformity that supersedes those laws for a planned time period to accomplish a higher and more personal purpose for God. The following illustration will show how these things work.

Law of Aerodynamics vs. Law of Gravity

When I travel to different nations, I usually go by plane. Those planes weigh numerous tons and carry hundreds of people. There is a law of gravity that says anything in the air that is heavier than the air will fall to the ground. But I get on that jet with several hundred other people. We buckle up, the plane picks up speed down the runway for about 45 seconds and then all that weight of plane and people goes into the air to about 38,000 feet, levels off and stays in the air for about fifteen hours until I reach my destination.

How does the plane fly that high and then maintain its place in the air when the law of gravity says it should fall to the ground? The overpowering law of aerodynamics is superseding the law of gravity. It does not do away with the law of gravity or change its truthful reality. The working principle of gravity still remains as true and effective as it has always been since God set it in motion when He created the earth.

The Law of Transformation and Process for Conformity of humankind to the likeness of Christ do not lessen or do away with God's will for humankind to have all the blessings He promised for His children's natural lives. God showed His will for humankind to be blessed when He placed Adam and Eve in the Garden of Eden where everything they could need or desire was available. What Jesus provided for His Church when He was crucified, buried and resurrected is still valid and available to all who will believe and receive.

We will probably not know all the reasons God created humans in His own image and likeness until we are in heaven with Christ Jesus. Nevertheless, we will discover several of the reasons in this book as we reveal the main processes God uses to conform His chosen ones into beings just like Him. To most Christians it sounds impossible that we can come to the fullness and maturity of Christ Jesus. That is one reason God made humans in His own likeness: so they would have the capability to mature to the place of thinking like and functioning like God. Jesus made the way for us to be partakers of His divine nature and attributes (see 2 Peter 1:4).

Jesus Made the Way

Jesus came to earth as a man to make a way for Father God and humankind to be united together in fellowship once again—the God-man Jesus is forming a God-like people. Jesus was God manifested in a human body. His coming to the earth and shedding His blood made the way for Jew and Gentile to be one new family. Jesus also made a way for Himself to be joined with His Bride. God the Son is the Head, and His redeemed people are His corporate Body.

God was working through Jesus' obedience to reconcile redeemed humankind unto Himself—not just to a place but to a Person. All the glory and praise go to Jesus Christ who made it all possible for God's plans for humankind to be fulfilled and for humankind to fulfill God's highest calling for His people.

ACKNOWLEDGMENT & PETITION

The illustration of the thumb representing the inward man and the four fingers representing all things of our natural temporary life is the best illustration for understanding how the Law of Transformation and the Process for Conformity works and makes sense. The laws of prosperity, healing and all other blessings promised are not lessened but superseded by a higher purpose of God. Lord Jesus, help me keep my priorities in alignment with Yours. Help me keep the attitude that "the sufferings of this present time are not worthy to be compared with the glory/Christlikeness that shall be revealed in me." I acknowledge that it will be worth it all!

8

When Loss Is Gain

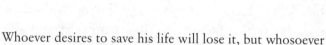

Whoever desires to save his life will lose it, but whosoever loses his life for My sake and the gospel's will save it. For what will it profit a man if he gains the whole world, and loses his own soul?

Mark 8:35–36

Yes, our outward man can suffer the loss of some natural things, but our inward man gains valuable things that are spiritual and eternal. Jesus amplified this truth in Mark 8:36–37: "What will it profit a man if he gains the whole world, and loses his own soul? Or what will a man give in exchange for his soul?"

Jesus is asking, "What are you willing to give up or lose in the natural life to gain in your spiritual and eternal life?" When Jesus has the Holy Spirit take us through a Process for Conformity, it may cost us something or the loss of something. What are we willing to lose if in the process it produces more of the Christlikeness within us? The apostle Paul declared that he was not only willing but had done it.

> What things were *gain* to me, these I have counted *loss* for Christ. Yet indeed I also count all things *loss* for the excellence of the knowledge of Christ Jesus my Lord, for whom I have suffered the *loss* of all things, and count them as rubbish, that I may *gain* Christ.
>
> Philippians 3:7–8, emphasis added

A man is wise to give up that which he cannot keep to gain that which he cannot lose. Paul forsook all he had obtained in education (becoming a doctor of the Law in the Jewish faith), favor with the high priest and all the high-standing officials, and positions he had attained in order to follow Christ Jesus. When young people who were Jewish or Muslim accepted Christ Jesus as their Savior, they were normally disowned by their parents. Early Christians in Rome lost their citizenship rights and sometimes their very lives.

In these verses Paul is not just talking about the willingness to suffer loss that comes with becoming a Christian, for this letter to the Philippians was written to Christians in the latter years of his life and ministry. He is talking about what he would give in exchange for his soul being conformed to the likeness of Jesus Christ. My prayer is that I have the revelation and dedication that Paul had, which enabled him to go through all he did to gain complete death to self and conformity to the image and likeness of Jesus. I pray, also, that this truth will be so born of God within your mind and spirit that it will enable you to go through whatever is required for you to be completely conformed to the likeness of Jesus Christ.

My Conforming Process: When Loss Was Gain

In December 1977, as I mentioned earlier, we moved Christian International from San Antonio, Texas, to Phoenix, Arizona. We caravanned ten families and all of CI's material in three 24-foot rental trucks, one large motor home, two vans and three cars. My wife and I had flown out earlier and bought a three-thousand-square-foot home on an acre of land. We built a two-thousand-square-foot building on the back of the property for office space.

After a year the neighbors complained because we had so many people driving on the gravel road and stirring up dust. The zoning commission said we were not zoned to have commercial business on the property but residential only. So we started looking for property and found an acre on Glendale Avenue that had a large house on it and several other buildings. The house had had a fire in it and was vacant. The people who owned it had used it as a headquarters for their religious group. They had moved back to Missouri where they owned eight hundred acres. The property was worth more than $200,000. They sold it to us for $150,000 with $30,000 down and the balance of the $120,000 to be paid in three yearly payments of $40,000 with no interest charges.

We had no extra money in those days, and we were new in the area and were not able to finance the balance. One of my ministers had sold his home and sowed $50,000 to CI as a firstfruits offering. We used $30,000 for the down payment and the remainder to repair the damaged areas in the house and the cottages. Leon Walters and his family moved from Denver, Colorado, to Phoenix and moved in with us. Leon was a contractor of interior finishing with Sheetrock and painting. By way of background, Leon had married Donna, my wife's younger sister, in 1962. They moved back to San Antonio, Texas, to attend International Bible College. Evelyn's dad and mom moved from Washington State to attend the same college. In 1964 I was invited to come and teach at the Bible college. Leon and my mother-in-law were in their third year of college. I was one of their teachers for that year.

Leon began working on the interior of the house we had bought, and I began my itinerate preaching. I traveled and preached in many churches, and in several of the churches I mentioned our need for money to make the payments. Only one church took an offering for the building. We were given $5,000—that was all we had toward the first payment when it came due in March 1979. The owners gave us a ninety-day extension, but still no money. They gave another extension until September, but that would be the last extension. If payment was not made, then they would repossess the property.

I tried everything. They would not change the payment schedule. The banks would not loan us money. I tried to make deals with people if they helped me pay off the mortgage. It was a dead-end street everywhere I turned. God opens doors that no man can shut, and He closes doors that no man can open. And this man could not open any door to make the payment. God shut every door.

In September I had to sign all the property back to them with all the money and improvements we had invested. We had to move CI off the property.

My Personal Gethsemane

This Process did not affect my wife as it did me. It hit me hard in several ways. My spiritual son and minister had given CI the $50,000 from the sale of his home—and I lost it and the property. It affected me as a minister: I could not believe God for the money to come in—I was a failure as a man of God. I was just getting involved with the faith movement. I thought that with God supplying the $50,000, it would be no problem for us to believe for a $40,000 payment.

I beat myself up, disqualified myself and condemned myself. I did the devil's work for him. I descended into the Elijah pit of desperate discouragement and disqualification. I felt like praying to die, but I couldn't. We were conducting the School of the Holy Spirit every Friday night with several hundred people attending. I would preach to the people about the prophetic and gifts of the Spirit. I would then prophesy to individuals until after midnight, sometimes until two o'clock in the morning. People would get saved, healed and activated for ministry and rejoice greatly over the prophecies they received.

Then I would go back home and crawl into my pit of hopeless despair. It was a very challenging and confusing time. I had heard the saying, "When you are down to nothing, God is up to something." I was definitely down to nothing, but I had no idea what God was up to.

Six Months of Silence from God

For six months God would *speak through me* but *not to me*. Evelyn and I traveled several hundred miles looking for property that we could buy for CI headquarters. One night we were traveling back from Tucson to Phoenix. We stopped at a motel to spend the night. I told my wife I was going to take a walk underneath the bright starlit sky. During those six months, I had not heard a word from the Lord concerning the property—no enlightenment as to why we lost it and no confirmation as to whether we should buy more property or keep renting.

What do you do during times like this when you have done everything you know to do and still you have seemingly lost and failed? Do what Paul said in Ephesians 6:10–17: Put on the whole armor of God; stand steadfast; and keep pressing on till God is ready to speak. When it is dark and you cannot see clearly, do not doubt in the dark what God showed you in the light. Even when the dark clouds hide the sun, it is still shining, right on time and moving ahead on schedule.

When you are going through a Job experience it is good to read the book of Job and discover how he made it when he had lost it all—his children, possessions, health, reputation and popular position in the community. All he had left around him were three criticizing friends and his wife who was of no encouragement. She told him to curse God and die.

Job answered her by saying, "You speak like a foolish woman. We have accepted God's prosperity and health; shall we not accept the adversity that He has allowed to come upon us?"

In all Job's two-year-long trial he did not sin with his lips. When the servants came and reported that everything of his had been either stolen or killed, including his ten children when a tornado hit the four corners of their house, when Job heard it all, he shaved his head, put on his mourning clothes and sat down in a pile of ashes and said with his mouth: "The Lord has given, and the Lord has taken away; blessed be the name of the Lord."

When Satan came back the second year, God again challenged Satan regarding Job just as He had the first time. Only this time, Satan accused Job of caring about nothing but his own skin. Satan got permission to afflict his body. Satan struck Job with painful boils from the top of his head to the soles of his feet. After weeks of suffering and his three friends trying to convince Job that he must have sinned or done something wrong for him to be going through his horrible situation, Job defended himself.

He declared, "God is not talking to me, and I cannot see Him or sense His presence. But I fully believe that He knows the way that I take. And *when He has finished testing me, I shall come forth as gold*. I have treasured the words of His mouth more than my necessary food. For He performs what is appointed for me" (see Job 23:8–14).

Do you know who in the Bible is the man upon whom God put the most honor and trust? Job! God challenged Satan with Job saying, "I have a man who fears Me. He loves Me and is a virtuous and upright man, and I find no fault in him." God conveyed, "I have blessed him all his life with health, wealth and prestige. He is the wealthiest and most honored man in all the East. He loves me more than he loves his family, wealth and honor. Nothing you can do, Satan, to Job could cause him to lose faith in Me and his commitment to My way of life."

The contest was on. Who would be proved right: God or Satan? God risked His reputation by putting His faith in a man. Job won the contest for God by staying true to Him. God was proven right in His knowledge and wisdom and trust in His man, Job. I wonder how much God trusts us. Talk about faith in God—how about God's faith in man?

Nevertheless, it was greatly stressful and trying to Job when he could not hear from God during the Process. God finally spoke to Job in chapter 38.

God Finally Speaks to Me!

As I was walking and praying, God started talking to me.

He said, *Bill Hamon, you seem to be really upset and frustrated about the property and the money.*

I said, "Yes, I am. I lost all that money and property, and it was the money that my spiritual son gave to me. I don't know why You are still blessing people through me since I am such a failure. I lost it all." I did not blame God for not supplying; I blamed myself for not having had the faith to produce the payment.

God then surprised me by saying to me, *Bill Hamon, you did not lose anything.*

(I thought to myself, *God, have You been on vacation for the last six months? It's all gone!*)

I said to the Lord, "I had to sign the property with all the labor and money we had put into it back over to the owner."

He said again to me, *You did not lose that money!*

"Okay, Lord, You need to explain how it is that I didn't lose anything."

He said, *That money and property are the tuition that I was willing to pay for the wisdom and maturity that this Process is producing in you. I had to develop this in you before I could launch you into the next revelation and ministry in your destiny.*

To help me understand and to show me how serious He was, Jesus said something that made a believer out of me.

Jesus said, *If the property had been as valuable as the Oral Roberts University and grounds, I still would have sacrificed it for you to receive the wisdom and maturity in Christ-likeness that you will need for the next level of ministry I have planned for you to fulfill for Me. I can give you houses, lands and people overnight, but I cannot give you wisdom and maturity overnight—that requires a Process.*

I thought about this.

"Okay, Lord," I said, "if that was Your tuition money invested for my wisdom and maturity in You, and I didn't lose it, then I release all failure and condemnation from myself. I receive Your joy, Lord, and the peace of God. Forgetting those things that are behind me, I will press on toward my highest calling of continually being conformed into Your image and likeness."

The Gain: More of Christ's Wisdom and Maturity

My *loss* of natural and temporary things was my *gain* of divine, eternal things. It was a conforming Process that made my loss my gain. Can loss be gain? Yes! When it is a God-ordained Process to work into us the nature and character of Jesus Christ. Only God can make our traumas, tragedies, tests, trials and afflictions work for us the far greater *good* of being transformed into the likeness of Christ Himself.

The apostle John declared this in 1 John 5:4: "For whatever is born of God overcomes the world." You can let this truth impregnate your soul: Get pregnant with it, and let it grow within you until it can be born of God to be your way of life.

When you experience the joys, blessings and benefits of being conformed to the Christ-life, you will be able to say with the conviction that Paul did, "I consider that the sufferings of this present time are not worthy to be compared with the glory [Christlikeness] which shall be revealed in us" (Romans 8:18).

Heaven Is Waiting for Our Completed Process

There are several groups in heaven waiting for this conforming Process to be accomplished, for it will have direct effect upon them.

Romans 8:18, quoted just above, talks about the glory that shall be revealed after conformity to Christlikeness is accomplished in the chosen saints. Verse 19 reveals, "For the earnest expectation of the creation *eagerly waits* for the revealing of the sons of God" (emphasis added). The revealing and manifestation of the Christlike sons of God starts a chain reaction that affects the whole Creation, "because the creation itself also will be delivered from the bondage of corruption into the glorious liberty of the children of God" (verse 21).

Not only is all creation waiting, but we who have the firstfruits of the Spirit are also eagerly waiting for the adoption, the redemption of our bodies from mortal to immortal-eternal (see Romans 8:23).

There is another group waiting for this Christlikeness to be fulfilled—for they will not be perfected apart from us—the *heroes of faith* and the great *cloud of witnesses* who have lost their human bodies through death, but are waiting until this occasion that we have been learning about is fulfilled. They will then have the redemption of their bodies by the resurrection of the dead. They will be perfected by having their eternal spirit, soul and immortalized bodies united, never to be separated again. (See Hebrews 11:40; 12:1; 1 Corinthians 15:53; 1 Thessalonians 4:16.)

There is another who has been waiting a long time until a certain thing happens. Jesus has been sitting at the right hand of the Father ever since He rose from the dead and ascended to heaven and birthed His Church; He sat down at the right hand of God and is waiting until His enemies are made His footstool (see Acts 3:21; Hebrews 10:13). Whom is Jesus waiting on to make His enemies His footstool? His corporate Body, His Church, which He is perfecting in His own likeness and ministry. Jesus has predestined the Church to fulfill all prophetic Scriptures right up to the prophetic Scriptures concerning our resurrection-translation at His personal return.

ACKNOWLEDGMENT & PETITION

You have proven to me, Lord, that a committed Christian predestined for Your purpose does not have problems but predestined purposes that produce Christlikeness. What seems to be failure is just Your process for fulfillment. All things—success and failure, popularity and criticism, friends and enemies—all things are for the sake of conforming me to Christlikeness. So I can rejoice evermore and in all things give thanks. Since God is for me, nothing and no one can be against me. Jesus, make this truth so born of God within me that nothing can deter me from fulfilling all You have purposed for my life. Your joy will continually be my strength!

9

Conforming to Jesus' Ability to Forgive

[Jesus said,] "But if you do not forgive, neither will your Father in heaven forgive your trespasses."

Mark 11:26

From talking to Christian counselors, pastors and Christian psychologists and from my own experience counseling, I have discovered one of the greatest weaknesses in Christians. It is the inability to forgive as Christ forgives.

Therefore, as the elect of God, holy and beloved, put on tender mercies, kindness, humility, meekness, longsuffering; bearing with one another, and *forgiving* one another, if anyone has a complaint against another; *even as Christ forgave you, so you also must do.*

Colossians 3:12–13, emphasis added

The Scriptures exhort us to forgive others freely as Christ Jesus has freely forgiven us. Even the Lord's Prayer that Jesus taught His disciples to pray includes forgiving others: "Forgive us our debts/trespasses, as we forgive our debtors/trespassers." *As* implies that we are asking the Lord to forgive us to the same degree as we forgive others. Just as I forgive others, Jesus, forgive me the same way.

The Unforgivable Sin of Unforgiveness

Jesus told His disciples a story that emphasizes this truth.

> Peter came to [Jesus] and said, "Lord, how often shall my brother sin against me, and I forgive him? Up to seven times?"
>
> Jesus said to him, "I do not say to you, up to seven times, but up to seventy times seven. Therefore the kingdom of heaven is like a certain king who wanted to settle accounts with his servants. And when he had begun to settle accounts, one was brought to him who owed him ten thousand talents [millions of dollars today]. But as he was not able to pay, his master commanded that he be sold, with his wife and children and all that he had, and that payment be made. The servant therefore fell down before him, saying, 'Master, have patience with me, and I will pay you all.' Then the master of that servant was moved with compassion, released him, and forgave him the debt.
>
> "But that servant went out and found one of his fellow servants who owed him a hundred denarii [a few dollars]; and he laid hands on him and took him by the throat, saying, 'Pay me what you owe!' So his fellow servant fell down at his feet and begged him, saying, 'Have patience with me, and I will pay you all.' And he would not, but went and

threw him into prison till he should pay the debt. So when his fellow servants saw what had been done, they were very grieved, and came and told their master all that had been done. Then his master, after he had called him, said to him, 'You wicked servant! I forgave you all that debt because you begged me. Should you not also have had compassion on your fellow servant, just as I had pity on you?' And his master was angry, and delivered him to the torturers until he should pay all that was due to him.

"So My heavenly Father also will do to you if each of you, *from his heart*, does not *forgive* his brother his trespasses."

Matthew 18:21–35, emphasis added

Jesus gave this illustration to reveal to us what His heavenly Father will do to us if we do not forgive others from our hearts. He will turn us over to demonic torturers until we do forgive from our hearts the ones who did us wrong. Biblical *forgiveness* must come from *the heart*—not be just verbal or soulish but rise from the depth of our beings, our hearts. In fact, Jesus declared that His heavenly Father could not and would not forgive us our sins unless we first forgave those who sinned against us.

In this story the master of all the servants represents God, and the servants are God's people. Does that mean if we still have unforgiveness in our hearts toward others when we stand before the Judgment Seat of Christ that we will be standing there with unforgiven sins in the record of our time on earth? In this chapter, I want to share with you how the Law of Transformation using the Process for Conformity taught me to forgive as Christ Jesus forgives.

Transferred to Teaching at a Bible College

From fall 1964 until spring 1969 my ministry was that of professor at a Bible college in San Antonio, Texas. Before I came to teach at the college, most of my ministry and Bible reading had focused on the New Testament. But at the Bible college, though I did teach the book of Romans for three years as well as the prison epistles, my assignment was mainly to teach the books of the Old Testament. During the five years I was there I taught all the books of the Old Testament in their groupings: the first five books of the Bible called the Pentateuch, the twelve historical books, the five poetic books, the five major prophets and the twelve minor prophets. Those categories include all 39 books of the Old Testament. It had a very broadening effect on my knowledge of the Bible.

These five years of Bible college, while I was teaching and we were living on the campus with our three children, were our most carefree and enjoyable years. Our children were ages seven, five and three when we arrived. I had just turned thirty when we moved from Washington State to San Antonio. I mention this because it is significant: It finalized an arrangement I had made with the Lord.

But First, Some Tests and Trials

In 1961 we had been traveling in ministry for a year when my wife became pregnant. By the time she was four months along she began developing serious problems to the extent she could hardly move about. I had to stop traveling in ministry and get a secular job so that I could take care of her and our two sons. We were visiting with my dad and mom, who were living in Amarillo, Texas, at that time. By the time Evelyn was seven months along, she could not sit up or lie down because of the knots and spasms in her stomach.

One night God gave me a dream of Him throwing a lariat around us and swinging us back to Yakima, Washington. God was telling us to move immediately. We loaded our little sixteen-foot trailer house and hooked it up to our 1954 Plymouth, which had 150,000 miles on it. We began driving the sixteen hundred miles through the mountainous country to Yakima. When we arrived, I took Evelyn to see the doctor who had delivered Tim and Tom.

After he examined my wife, he said he saw no chance for the baby being born alive and a 50/50 chance for the mother making it through a delivery. She had a severe case of preeclampsia and her creatine was way too high. He changed her whole diet, which was different from the one the doctor in Texas had her on. He said he would have to take the baby four weeks early if things did not change.

But, thank God, through much prayer and faith decreeing the baby came forth six weeks early weighing just four pounds and twelve ounces, and did not even have to be put in an incubator. We named our little miracle girl Sherilyn Yvonne Hamon. Her mom also came through victoriously.

Winter Season of Confusion

From the time our daughter was born May 13, 1961, until we left for San Antonio, Texas, on my thirtieth birthday on July 29, 1964, I worked in the business world. Why am I sharing this with you concerning what was happening in my life before teaching at the Bible college? Because it has a definite part in God's fulfilling His purpose for my life.

Being out of full-time ministry made me feel as if I were out of my calling and just marking time. I had been in ministry all my adult life since I was nineteen years old. I felt like Joseph being out of his home country and away from his family. I had to die to the ministry. It was a heartbreaking challenge and test to think I might never return to preaching.

In order to eliminate my constant confusion and frustration, I presented a proposition to God. I said to God, "Since I no longer know whether I am to be a preacher or a businessperson, here is what I am settling on. I remember what You told me when I was in my early twenties, that wherever I was and whatever I was doing in my thirtieth year would be my calling for the rest of my life. Lord, I am settling on this. Whatever I am doing in my thirtieth year, whether in the preaching ministry or the business world, I will accept that as my life's work for the rest of my life."

Two years later, in January 1964, I received an invitation to come to Texas to be a teacher at a Bible college. I told them I could not come that semester, but I would be able to begin in the fall semester. We could not leave right then for we had to settle an insurance claim regarding damages my wife received in a car accident while riding with another woman. The car had flipped over three times, and my wife's third, fourth and fifth vertebrae were crushed; she was receiving therapy three times a week.

We would have to wait until she was well enough to travel before we could make the journey. Thank God we received the insurance settlement, paid off debts, bought a nice station wagon and Evelyn was healed enough to travel. When

I turned thirty, we were on our way for me to be a full-time minister, preaching and teaching young people to be ministers of the Gospel of Jesus Christ. My future calling and destiny were settled. I was to be a minister of Jesus Christ revealing His Process for building His Church and transforming and maturing His children into the likeness of His Son, Jesus Christ.

Things I Learned through the Process

There were several things I learned through God's Process for Conformity to the Christ-way of thinking and living. When I had to die to my vision of ministry and great accomplishments, God taught me that He had called me to be His minister to fulfill His purpose, not my ambitious desires. The apostle Paul said that God "made me a minister"; Jesus revealed that He was in the process of making Bill Hamon the kind of minister He wanted him to be. My position in life did not determine my ministerial calling, whether in a pulpit or in a car with a salesman's briefcase. David was God's chosen vessel whether he was killing giants, running from Saul or sitting on the throne of Israel.

Our position and type of performance may change many times in our lifetimes, but the calling is the same 24/7—every day from the original calling to the ultimate fulfillment at the end of our days. God keeps the ultimate purpose and destiny for our lives before Him, not our moment-by-moment position and performance. I had to learn to do the same. Joseph was as much in the will and timing of God in His Process of fulfilling His purpose for Joseph's life when he was in jail as when he was positioned next to Pharaoh to rule the great Egyptian empire. The apostle Paul was still in full-time ministry the several times he was in jail writing letters to the churches. Those letters became books of the Bible. He probably would not have had time to write the fourteen letters if he had been continuously traveling in ministry. What seemed to be his limitation in jail became our liberation in all the truths he made available to the Body of Christ.

God does not always put value and importance on things the way we do. The journey to fulfilling our destinies is as important to God as the arrival. For it is in our journeys that the Law of Transformation and the Process for Conformity are accomplishing God's highest calling in our lives—becoming God's kind of man or woman, continually being conformed to the image and likeness of Jesus Christ.

The Process develops within us the nature and character of Christ and gives us revelation of God's ways. Psalm 103:7 states that God showed Israel His *acts*, but He revealed His *ways* to Moses. Knowing Jesus means more than knowing His truth and life; it also means knowing His ways, for Jesus is the way, the truth and the life (see John 14:6).

False Accusations Hit Home

This brings us back to the Bible college situation where God taught me His way of forgiveness by putting me through a Process for Conformity until I received the revelation and grace to be able to forgive others as Jesus had forgiven me.

After five years of teaching at the college and the graduation exercises for the students in May 1969, Evelyn and I were packing and preparing for our summer itinerate ministry. We were looking forward to returning at the end of August to resume my work at the college.

A few days before we were to leave with our three children for the summer, our daughter, eight years old now, came into the house with an envelope in her hand. She said that the president of the college had given a letter to her out on the sidewalk and told her to give it to her dad.

Evelyn and I read the letter with shock and dismay. The president of the college had his wife type the letter, which said, basically, "Please do not come back to the school this fall, for you are being dismissed from your position. Please remove your possessions from the house, as others will be occupying it in the fall. You are being removed because of insubordination and teaching the 'never die' false doctrine."

This was the essence of what the letter said. I never did find out what I had supposedly done to be guilty of insubordination. I did find out why he accused me of false doctrine.

I learned that he had listened on the intercom, which he had in every classroom, and had heard me say something about the "never die" doctrine. I was teaching the class about some of the false doctrines that arose in the Latter Rain movement, and one of those was the "never die" doctrine. The extreme teaching was taken from Jesus' words that if you would eat His flesh and drink His blood you would never die. They also based the teaching on the Scripture that says Jesus took the keys of death from the devil and gave them to the Church, giving believers the key to unlock the power of death and personally go to heaven without dying.

Latter Rain taught that if you had the faith Enoch exercised, you could defy death and go to heaven like Enoch and Elijah and "never die." Hebrews 11:5 declares that "by faith

Enoch was taken away so that he did not see death"—he was translated to heaven. From this they presented what is called a half-truth—the Scripture is true, but man's interpretation, application, timing and method for fulfillment of the Scripture was false.

I believe that the college president was looking for an excuse to get rid of me, so when he heard me say "never die," he grabbed it as evidence that I was teaching a false doctrine. Without clarification, he accused me of being guilty of promoting error and dismissed me.

Traveling Ministry, Looking for Open Doors

We stored our household stuff and headed out on our journey for the summer, and we knew not where we might be in the fall. One of our first meetings was in Sarnia, Ontario, Canada. On the way there we talked much about what had just happened. I felt the president of the college had released me contrary to the will of God. I had been told by the Lord that my life would progress similarly to the way David's did. David was seven years ruling in Hebron, and then he moved on to greater prophetic fulfillment. I figured we would be there at the college for seven years and then be moved on to fulfill prophetic destiny. I reasoned that because of the president's fears, jealousy and not being enthused with me being a prophet and my prophetic ministry, he had dismissed me two years ahead of God's timing for my life and ministry.

Before we left, I wrote a letter to all the students and the ministers I knew and had preached with over the years to let them know why I would not return to the college.

I wrote twelve pages.

Evelyn read it and said, "Honey, you don't need to say all of that."

I rewrote it down to six pages. I showed it to her and got the same response.

I finally reduced it down to two pages. I basically eliminated all the details of who, what, when, where and why and wrote that we had come to a parting of the ways like Paul and Barnabas, David and Saul. At that time, I was so upset and not sanctified enough and had such insufficient revelation of God's Process that I had to make the point that I was likened to Paul and David, and he was likened to Barnabas and Saul. I included 2 Samuel 3:1: "David grew stronger and stronger, and the house of Saul grew weaker and weaker."

Even though it all proved true over the next 35 years, at the time I did not have enough revelation and maturity to maintain a proper attitude and response that a man of God should demonstrate during a Process like that. But we all do the best we can with what we have and who we are during our time of processing.

Being Transformed in Nature and Character

We continue to grow and go from glory to glory—Christlikeness to more Christlikeness and maturity. I did not know at that time as I know now that the college president was my "friend" and "employee" working to build the character of Christ within me—especially the character of blessing those who make my life miserable and forgiving them when they do, showing long-suffering and endurance, loving those who do not manifest love to me, and being like Jesus to those who were crucifying Him when He said,

"Father, forgive them, for they do not know what they do" (Luke 23:34).

That is one reason I am writing this book, so that all of you young'uns under eighty years old can learn these truths and overcoming principles early and be able to go through God's processes with greater revelation, faith and a continual forgiving attitude toward people and circumstances. Maybe you will even be able to do what the apostle James said to do when all kinds of trials and temptations crowd into your life: Welcome them as friends. Maybe you will even do what Paul said to do: Believe it is all working together for your good, rejoice evermore and in all things give thanks for this is the will of God in Christ Jesus concerning you. Maybe you can take out some money and pay your "employees" for the great work they are doing in your life—for all afflictions and afflicters are working for you.

You are in the driver's seat; drive on rejoicing! As Paul conveyed, I just forget those people and things, leaving them behind, setting my eyes on the goal of being Christlike and pressing on with all I am and have, accomplishing that purpose Father God has predestined for my life.

While in Sarnia I prayed for hours during the day, asking the Lord to help me be able to forgive my Christian brother, the president of the college who had dismissed me from my ministry to all those young people. I was finally able to confess and forgive verbally, saying, "Lord, I forgive him for all he has done to me and my family."

Our Process Enables Us to Help Others

In the 1950s there was a chorus that we sang often about smoothing out the road to glory to make it easier for those following behind. I doubt if we can smooth out the road of life to where you do not have to go through God's Process for Conformity, but you can accept the wisdom, revelation, understanding and grace to go more smoothly through the Law of Transformation and the Process for Conformity.

One person expressed this thought: "I believe in faith confession, and I confess that I do not have to go through tests and trials." If you are going to submit to the Process of being conformed to the likeness of Christ, then you can confess your way through, but you cannot confess yourself around and avoid it. I trust this book will provide what you need to understand why we go through trials and tests to be transformed to the likeness of Christ. Most of all I pray that it will enable you to fulfill God's highest calling for your life. It will be worth all that we have to go through if we hear those most important words from Jesus: "Well done, good and faithful servant, enter into the eternal joy of the Lord."

God Positions Us for Finalizing the Process

We traveled on to the Northeast, and in New York we stopped and ministered in a Bible college with the hopes that they might offer me a position. We were praying and believing that God would provide something or someplace for us to fulfill our ministry without having to go back to Texas.

That did not happen. We arrived back in San Antonio and rented a house on the north side of the city. The house was surrounded by lots of trees, and Evelyn found it oppressive. We started looking for a home. We saw an ad in the paper about being able to buy a home without a down payment and having four months before making a house payment. Since we had no money for a down payment or a job to make house payments, we checked it out. We went and looked at it, bought it and moved in. After we moved in and started driving around, we discovered we were living just over a hill from the college where I had taught for five years.

I took a job at a commercial building downtown where I also located our Christian International Correspondence College. I had started building CI in 1968, a year before I was dismissed from the college. We enrolled our first student in the fall of 1968. In the fall of 1970, we established our first Christian International Extension College in the Philippines and in San Antonio.

I had to drive right by the college on my way to the commercial building where I worked to earn a living for my family. I was also working on building the extension college. Every time I drove past that Bible college, sadness and frustration would rise up within me.

I would think to myself, *If it weren't for the smallness of the president of the college, I would be there teaching and ministering to those young people.* I gradually got to the place in my soul where I did not get as emotional about it. I would repeat what I prayed in Sarnia as I drove by: "Lord, I forgive that man for all the heartache and frustration he has caused me." Nevertheless, I was still holding judgment against him and condemning him for his actions.

Discovering Three Levels of Forgiveness

A year later as I was driving by the college, God spoke to me and said to pull over and park for a moment.

He asked me if I was still upset about the whole situation. *Do you feel unjustly wronged?*

I said, "Yes!"

Jesus asked, *What can I do to make you feel vindicated? Do you want Me to have the college burn down? Do you want Me to strike him blind?* Jesus said it in such a way that He made me believe He was serious.

I thought about it for a while. It would not help me if Jesus did either of those things.

Jesus said, *Why don't you just go ahead and forgive him? From your heart?*

"Lord, I forgave him with my mouth in Sarnia, and I forgave him while driving by this place."

Yes, He said, *you have forgiven with your lips and some with your emotions, but you have not forgiven from your heart. My Father requires complete forgiveness just as He forgives and I forgive. You must remove from your heart and mind all judgments against him, all accusations of wrongdoing. You must eradicate every negative feeling you have toward him.*

"Lord, I don't know how or if I can do that."

If you are willing, He said, *I will give you My ability to forgive completely.*

I shook my head. "I don't know if I am worthy to receive Your ability."

The ability that I am talking about is not earned; it is freely given just because you ask. The grace that I am talking about is My unmerited divine ability. It is the same grace you were saved by.

I knew the verse he was referring to: "By grace you have been saved through faith, and that not of yourselves; it is the gift of God" (Ephesians 2:8).

I finally grasped what divine forgiveness really is. It makes you feel even better than you did before the offense happened. When you think about what happened you feel as though it happened to someone else; remembering the thoughts of what happened no longer has a negative effect within you.

One reason it makes you feel so good, clear and clean is because when you truly forgive others from your heart, then God can forgive you fully, which is the Scripture we quoted at the beginning of this chapter—if we do not forgive others from our hearts, then God cannot and will not forgive us our trespasses and sins. When we remove all judgment, blame, hurt feelings and accusations from our hearts, it does not release the guilty from their wrong attitudes and actions. But it does set us free and bring inner healing to our wounded spirits.

I discovered that, for deep wounds of wrongdoing from a person or an incident, it takes about a year to go through the three levels required to give biblical forgiveness from our hearts. We first forgive verbally because the Bible says we have to, whether someone has an offense against us or we have an offense against someone else. In the second level, we have forgiven enough until it does not affect us as much. We bury the hatchet, so to speak, but we leave the handle sticking out to remind us what the person did—and if they ever do it again, we can pull the hatchet out and use it on them.

But for us to reach the third level, biblical forgiveness must be with our whole body, soul and spirit:

body = speech
soul = emotions
spirit = heart

It is like the biblical standards Jesus gave us for loving God. It must be accomplished with the whole body, soul and spirit; and we must love our neighbors as ourselves. We ask forgiveness from God, and then we give forgiveness to others, and we do it to the same depth as we expect Christ Jesus to forgive us.

Is It Worth It All?

Was it worth the Process for Conformity that involved being fired unjustly, having to leave the ministry and work in a secular job with sales meetings in cigarette smoke–filled rooms, feeling used and abused and being disqualified from full-time ministry, which is the love of my life?

Yes! It was worth it all. When I look back and see all that the Lord was doing for my inner spirit and eternal man, I can say it was worth it. I was transformed and conformed much more to Christ's divine nature. The greatest aspect of it—Christ's divine nature to forgive—was worked into the very fiber of my inner being. It caused me to give every spare moment to building the Christian International School of Theology. CI grew to around nine thousand students around the world, with numerous CI extension colleges in numerous churches. CI made a way for me to be back in full-time spiritual ministry. It supported my family and ten other families and staff members. Evelyn and (possibly) I would never have wanted to leave teaching at the college, for we were so happy and fulfilled there. But God and His Process for Conformity orchestrated everything to transform us more into being like Jesus, especially in that all-important grace of forgiving from our hearts: the God-given ability to forgive as Christ Jesus forgives.

ACKNOWLEDGMENT & PETITION

Father, You seem to be very serious about forgiveness from the heart. You have made it the sin that cannot be forgiven unless we forgive those who have sinned against us. Holy Spirit, search the depths of my heart and make sure there is absolutely no unforgiveness there whatsoever. I cannot reach full conformity to the likeness of Christ Jesus if biblical forgiveness is not fully working within me. Thank You, Lord, for total forgiveness as I totally forgive others.

10

Marriage in the Conforming Process

"For this reason a man shall leave his father and mother and be joined to his wife, and the two shall become one flesh."

Ephesians 5:31 (see also Genesis 2:24)

There are several reasons why God created the mankind race as male and female. The number one reason was for the purpose of reproducing themselves. This enabled them to fulfill God's commission to fill the earth with a race in God's image and likeness.

Yet God had more in mind than just having a male and a female to reproduce another person. God, being the originator and creator of humankind, could have made man able to reproduce another person all by himself. But God did not do this for several reasons. God knew when He created Adam to be a free moral agent and able to function independently that man could disobey God's commands. He knew that greatest challenge for the independent self-life of man would be to submit his self-will to God's will, his thoughts and desires to God's. But God did not want man as a programmed machine or mechanical robot. He wanted living flesh-and-blood sons and daughters who would choose to love and obey Him. He gave them free will so they could freely, respectfully and lovingly relate to Him.

Self: The Problem vs. the Goal

God knew that man's problem would be *self*: self-centeredness, self-importance, self-concern, self-promotion; all forms of selfishness would be the biggest hindrance for maintaining God's image and likeness. God had watched the fall of Lucifer, which began with his self-concern and self-importance motivating him to try to throw God off His throne and establish himself as ruler of the universe and over all of God's creation. Selfishness can cause deception, delusions of grandeur and all kinds of irrational and unreasonable thinking. When you hear people expressing themselves that way you can be assured that they have a problem with self-centeredness. An unselfish person who has godly, sensible thoughts would call the selfish man's way of thinking ridiculous and stupid and likely say, "That's crazy, man!"

You can cast the demons of lust, fear, murder and other kinds of evil spirits out of people as Jesus did, but you cannot cast out the spirit of self-centeredness, for it is not a demon; it is the human spirit of the person. If you cast the spirit of self out, the person would be dead and gone out of his body. Lucifer did not have a demon or an evil spirit that needed to be cast out, for there was no such thing as evil and demons until Lucifer became the initiator and father of evil and demons. The blood of Jesus can cleanse you from all your sins and your demons, but you still have the new you to deal with.

Now some will say, "But I am a born-again new creation in Christ."

Yes. You are a new person, but you are still you with your free will to choose to be selfish or unselfish, righteous or unrighteous, self-centered or God-centered, living your own selfish life or submitting to being transformed into living the Christ-life. Adam was a new creation from the hand of God, but he chose to be unrighteous by disobeying God's commands. The Christ in you cannot sin, but the new you as a born-again mortal person can commit the sins originating from selfishness.

The main purpose for sharing this information is to reveal to you that you can think thoughts and take actions that are not inspired of God and that are not suggestions from the devil. God created man's self in His own self-image and likeness, which gave man his own creative ability to think and act on his own.

Marriage: The Ideal Place to Decrease Selfishness

I sometimes share with couples and those planning on getting married these thoughts: "God brings a man and woman together in marriage who have opposite backgrounds, personalities and lifestyles to perfect each other, but He gives them enough love for each other so that they do not kill one another in the Process." This is especially true with Christians who are destined to the Process for Conformity to the likeness of Jesus Christ. To have a successful Christian marriage, both husband and wife must submit to God's Process for Conformity to the likeness of Jesus.

My wife and I had a marriage relationship better than that of any other couple I have ever known. All 59 years were worth the living. We had a very good, compatible love life and working relationship. We both had the same ideas about having and raising our children. We both had the calling and commission to be ordained ministers of Jesus Christ.

But we had enough differences that at times we were each other's best "friend" and "employee." I was from the Deep South, and she was from the far Northwest. I was raised without ever going to a church. Evelyn was raised in church. She was saved when she was three and baptized in water and then with the Holy Spirit when she was seven.

I was born and raised in Oklahoma on a farm five miles from Red River, which is the borderline between Texas and Oklahoma. The area was real country; we walked over two miles to attend a two-room country school. We did not have electricity in that part of the country until I was fifteen years old. Evelyn thought she was raised "country" because they lived a mile outside of the little town of Zillah, Washington. But when she came to Oklahoma with me for a visit and found out my family lived without an inside or outside toilet, that was too prehistoric country for her. I had to drive her five miles into town to use a toilet.

Evelyn's dad was a sheepshearer by profession. He and his father and brothers would travel throughout Washington State and the surrounding states shearing thousands of sheep. He had bought a home on twenty acres with about twenty sheep and a couple of cows. They had to set sprinklers in the summertime to keep green grass for the animals. Evelyn was the oldest of a family of four girls. Her youngest, three-year-old sister was the flower girl in our wedding.

I was raised on a three-hundred-acre farm, where we grew peanuts, cotton and corn. We did not have tractors. We worked with mules and horses to get our work done. Fifty of the acres were a prairie grass field where we baled our hay for feed in the winter for our animals. The only heat we had for the house was a fireplace and a wood-burning cookstove. We drew our water from a cistern and later from a well, and took a weekly bath in a number-three-size washtub. All five of us children would take our baths in the same tub of water one after the other. As I said, we did not go to church. My dad had one religion: work, work, work, from sunup to sundown. He would take the whole family five miles to town once every week or so to buy groceries and go to the theater to see a Western movie, which was only shown once a week.

I met Evelyn when I started preaching a revival at her home church in February 1954, and we were married August 13, 1955. Evelyn married her pastor. The year after we were married, I brought my wife to Oklahoma to meet my family, whom she had never met. She decided that I was raised much more country than she was.

During our first years of marriage, we lived in the back of the church I was pastoring. It did not have bathroom or shower facilities. We had to walk to the front part of the church to use the toilets. The only heat we had for the winter was a portable electric heater and an electric blanket to keep us warm during the night. The stove was a wood burner, so we cooked with an electric skillet most of the time. There was no hot water unless we used the wood-burning cook-stove to heat some water from the cold-water faucet. But we were young (21 and 18), innocent, madly in love and so happy to be pastoring. We did not seem to be bothered by living in such rustic conditions.

Sowing Sacrifice Reaps Sufficiency

God appreciates it when we willingly go through suffering for the sake of Jesus and His Gospel. And He appreciates our willingness to give God His inheritance, which is the likeness of His Son, Jesus, in our lives and ministries. Remember, our key Scripture declares that God so desired our conformity to the life of Christ that *He predestined us to be conformed to the image of His Son so that Jesus might be the firstborn among many brethren.*

Father God has a special love and destiny for those of His children who have a passion to be like His Son and willingly submit to the Law of Transformation and go through God's Process for Conformity. That is one major reason the book of Job was included in the Bible—to give an example of how God chooses and rewards those who go through fiery trials in the Process until they come forth as pure gold. God rewards the latter years of their lives and gives back double to them all they lost in the Process. Look at these key statements.

My brethren, take the prophets, who spoke in the name of the Lord, as an example of suffering and patience. Indeed we count them blessed who endure. You have heard of the

perseverance of Job and seen the end intended by the Lord—
that the Lord is very compassionate and merciful.

James 5:10–11

The LORD restored Job's losses when he prayed for his friends
[they were the James 1:2–type of "friends"]. Indeed the LORD
gave Job twice as much as he had before. . . . Now the LORD
blessed the latter days of Job more than his beginning. . . .
After this Job lived one hundred and forty years, and saw his
children and grandchildren for four generations.

Job 42:10, 12, 16

God will bless those abundantly who persevere during
His Process for Conformity. This was true in the life of my
wife and me. During our early years, we sacrificed a lot and
suffered according to the will of God, going through His
processes. That was more applicable during our first thirty
years of ministry; things began to turn more to the rewards
and prosperity portion during the last thirty years of our
ministry.

In 1992 I was able to buy fifteen acres beside the church
property in Santa Rosa Beach, Florida. We developed it into
"Hamon Haven Subdivision" with nineteen one-half acre
lots. We named the half-mile-long street Hamon Avenue. My
wife and I gave one lot each to our children, and we took the
two-acre lot at the end of the road and built a home on it.
Each of our children built homes and raised their children
to grown-ups on Hamon Avenue. We now have four Hamon
families living on Hamon Avenue.

As with Job, God has blessed us in our latter days with
land, houses, eleven grandchildren and eighteen great-

grandchildren—which is our fourth generation, like Job. I am believing for a report like Job's of having a long life. I am believing for divine enablement to preach until I am at least 95 with health and energy to the end.

Jesus Promises a Hundredfold Return

Jesus emphasizes this principle in answering Peter's question.

> Then Peter began to say to [Jesus], "See, we have left all and followed You."
>
> So Jesus answered and said, "Assuredly, I say to you, there is no one who has left house or brothers or sisters or father or mother or wife or children or lands for My sake and the gospel's, who shall not receive a hundredfold now in this time—houses and brothers and sisters and mothers and children and lands, with persecutions—and in the age to come, eternal life."
>
> Mark 10:28–30

Notice Jesus said that those who sacrifice self to fulfill God's purpose in their lives will not only receive eternal rewards but will also be blessed a hundredfold now in this life. When you have spent much of your life sacrificing and suffering for Jesus, you really have to adjust to be able to receive God's hundredfold blessings without feeling a little guilty.

Successful Christian Marriages

I have done much marriage counseling in my many years of ministry. Most of these were Christian marriages. In addition,

I experienced and learned much in 59 years of marriage. I could give you numerous examples of how the relationship of marriage gives opportunity for the Process for Conformity to fulfill its God-appointed ministry to individual saints.

If you are married, especially if you have been married for some time, you also could list a dozen examples of where you had to die to some of your selfish pride and surrender to being conformed to the Christ-life. To have a successful marriage requires practicing the characteristics of Jesus as revealed in the love chapter of 1 Corinthians 13: learning to forgive as Jesus forgives, giving your mate the right to be him or herself, not always wanting to be right and have it all your way—this is essential for a long-lasting, enjoyable and successful marriage.

Self-Centeredness Destroys Marriages

I have seen again and again in marriage counseling that if one mate is so self-centered and self-opinionated that he (or she) cannot see his own faults and refuses to allow God to change him, it is impossible for the marriage to be joyful and successful. If the one partner refuses to make the adjustments that are required for a marriage to work, then that marriage is destined for divorce, or one of the mates will live in misery for the rest of his or her married life.

For the mate who wants the marriage to be one of joy, peace, love and fulfillment and feels that divorce is out of the question, then the only hope for a life worth living is to get the revelation that all of this is part of the processing to be transformed into the very life of Christ. If this is your situation, and that revelation becomes really born of God within you, then you can see your mate as your "employee" and "friend," causing you to be able to rejoice evermore, to be able to give thanks for all things, including your mate, to be able to bless those who curse you and do good to those who are making your life miserable. Then regardless of what kind of character your mate has, you are going to live your life with the joy of the Lord and the peace of God.

When we are transformed into living the life of Christ, then all His attributes, abilities and graces become active in our lives. Then our joy and peace in living are not dependent on what others do but on how we live the life of Christ, for He is our joy, love and purpose for living. If you are in such a situation, all this might sound impossible for your life. Remember that where sin and bad mates abound, God's grace (unmerited divine enablement) much more abounds (see Romans 5:20).

Sin Originated in Lucifer

Self-centeredness and selfishness will not be allowed to enter heaven and function there. It was the wrong thinking and motivation of self-importance in Lucifer that started the whole problem of sin. There was no such thing as sin and wrong self-motivation in God's entire universe and in all of heaven. There was no such thing in all creation of God's eternal beings of angels, cherubim and seraphim. God's universe and all creation had functioned for endless time without any rebellion or self-thoughts contrary to God's divine order.

But somewhere in the eternal past, the self-thought of rebellion and self-exaltation originated in the inner being of Lucifer.

Lucifer injected sin into God's human race when he manipulated Eve, the only woman on earth, to eat of the forbidden Tree of Knowledge of Good and Evil. Eve then gave the fruit to the only man on earth, Adam, her husband. Their selfish action, which was against God's divine order, activated sin into God's human race. God is concerned about the sins of unforgiveness and self-centeredness as much as any other sin that humans commit.

It was not the two major sins of murder and adultery that started the whole problem and horrible consequences of sin. All the problems of the world started with selfish pride. The prophet Isaiah reveals how Lucifer's thoughts created pride in him, causing him to set his will against God's will, resulting in his being cast out of heaven and into hell. "When the Son of Man comes in His glory . . . He will also say to those on the left hand, 'Depart from Me, you cursed, into the everlasting fire prepared for the devil and his angels'" (Matthew 25:31, 41).

"How you are fallen from heaven, O Lucifer, son of the morning! How you are cut down to the ground, you who weakened the nations! For you have said in your heart: '*I will* ascend into heaven, *I will* exalt my throne above the stars of God; *I will* also sit on the mount of the congregation on the farthest sides of the north; *I will* ascend above the heights of the clouds, *I will* be like the Most High.' Yet you shall be brought down to Sheol [hell], to the lowest depths of the Pit."

Isaiah 14:12–15, emphasis added

And war broke out in heaven: Michael and his angels fought with the dragon [Lucifer]; and the dragon and his angels

189

fought, but they did not prevail, nor was a place found for them in heaven any longer. So the great dragon was cast out, that serpent of old, called the Devil and Satan, who deceives the whole world; he was cast to the earth, and his angels were cast out with him.

Revelation 12:7–9

This shows the results of anyone who in selfish pride sets his or her will against God's will and divine order.

Raising Children Provides Further Opportunity

Marriage requires a reduction in self and so does raising a family. Each new child added to the family requires more of you. On the other hand, however, marriage and each child added can add more joy and fulfillment to your life—if you are living the Christ nature that gets joy out of serving others, and if you have learned the Christ-life principle that it is more blessed to give than to receive. Nevertheless, raising children can produce tests and trials. God uses them as "friends" and "employees" to help us go through the Process for Conformity as we allow the Law of Transformation to make us more into the likeness of Christ Jesus.

If you have not married or raised a family, God will use other means and opportunities to decentralize you from self and transform you into the likeness of Christ Jesus. God chooses the life situations that will best bring transformation in our lives. Remember the reality that during our first year of life we developed self-centeredness. After that it takes the Holy Spirit mostly the rest of our lives to decentralize us and transform our lives into the Christ-life.

I am so grateful for the privilege of having been married to my wonderful wife who helped us produce three children, who produced eleven grandchildren, who thus far have given us eighteen great-grandchildren. We were not only great lovers and best friends and dedicated parents, but at times were each other's "friend" and "employee," helping each other conform to the likeness of Christ Jesus. My wife must have reached her conformity, for the Lord took her on home. Jesus not only wanted me to do more work for Him but, evidently, wants to do more conforming in me.

That is the reason we can all say with David, the man after God's own heart, "My times are in Your hands, and not my timing and will be done but Your timing and will be accomplished in Your wisdom and purpose."

I am coming near the close of this book. My greatest desire and passion are that you will receive the revelation in these pages that will enable you to live more victoriously for the rest of your life. That you will be enlightened and encouraged to have a passionate dedication to fulfill God's highest calling for your life. That you will be one of those whom God sees as qualified to rule and reign as co-laborer with Christ throughout eternity.

ACKNOWLEDGMENT & PETITION

Lord Jesus, I thank You for these truths that have shown me what life is all about. It seems the number one purpose for life on earth is for me to be conformed to the likeness of God's Son, Jesus Christ, my Savior and Lord. Lord, I am thankful for the joys of my life, but

*now I realize that the difficult times were Your pro-
cesses working in my life. I give You thanks, therefore,
because I want to be like You more than anything else.
From this day forward, I will have a whole new attitude toward my family, my relationships and all that
happens in my life. I will live in confidence that it is
all working together for my good both for now and
eternally. Amen—so be it!*

11

What Christlikeness Looks Like

We shall be like Him [Jesus]. . . . Everyone who has this hope in Him purifies himself, just as He [Jesus] is pure. . . . Predestined to be conformed to image of [God's] Son [Jesus]. . . . [We] are being transformed into [His] same image from glory to glory.

1 John 3:2–3; Romans 8:29; 2 Corinthians 3:18

In this final chapter, we will seek to give a picture of what a person would be like in all areas of life when he or she has matured to Christlikeness. We stated earlier that Jesus was man's perfect God and God's perfect man. We will major in Jesus being God's perfect man, like the man God created Adam to be—in God's own image and likeness.

Before I began writing this chapter, I asked the Lord, "How am I going to give a thorough description of what a person would be like if he reached Christlikeness?"

The Holy Spirit started illuminating my mind with the following revelation. He reminded me of three passages of Scripture.

In the beginning was the Word, and the Word was with God, and the Word was God. . . . And the Word became flesh and dwelt among us, and we beheld His glory, the glory as of the only begotten of the Father, full of grace and truth.

John 1:1, 14

There are three that bear witness in heaven: the Father, the Word, and the Holy Spirit; and these three are one.

1 John 5:7

[Jesus said,] "I and My Father are one."

John 10:30

From these verses I realized that Jesus and the Word of God are the same. Also, Jesus the Word, the Father and the Holy Spirit are one. Whatever the Bible says about God the Father or the Holy Spirit, therefore, is a description of Jesus. Since the Word was made into the flesh, that made Jesus the walking, talking, living Word of God. That means the Bible, which is the written Word of God, contains all the descriptions of the attributes, characteristics and nature that Jesus was as the mortal man who was the Son of God. Jesus is the ideal model that God wants His Spirit-born sons of God to be like.

So all we have to do is go to the Word of God and find the biblical descriptions of what Jesus was and is in all areas of His life and ministry. From all these biblical descriptions, we will discover what a person will be like when he has been transformed into Christlikeness. Remember, the Bible never ever tells us to try to be like the Most High—the almighty, eternal God. For He is omnipresent, omniscient and omnipotent. Lucifer tried to be like God, and he was cast out of heaven.

I was preaching one time in 1956 in Bellingham, Washington. I was challenging the people to be like God.

The Holy Spirit spoke to me and said, *Do not tell them to be like God, but to be like His Son, Jesus Christ. There is no way that humans can ever be like God, but they can become like God's humankind Son.*

We can develop the godly attributes that Jesus demonstrated while a mortal man on earth. Jesus was God manifest in the flesh (see 1 Timothy 3:16). Jesus the Son of God was "the brightness of [God's] glory and the express image of His person" (Hebrews 1:3). Let's examine the Word of God to see what Christlikeness is like in the life of a man or woman of God.

Christlike in Character

The best explanation of Christ's character is found in the description of *love* in 1 Corinthians 13:4–8. I will use the New King James Version and another translation to give a full version of the description of love. Remember that God is love and love is God. This means that the love attributes are also the character of Christ Jesus.

Love suffers long and is kind; love does not envy; love does not parade itself, is not puffed up; does not behave rudely, does not seek its own, is not provoked, thinks no evil; does not rejoice in iniquity, but rejoices in the truth; bears all things, believes all things, hopes all things, endures all things. Love never fails.

Now I want to quote from the Phillips paraphrase, which is titled *The New Testament in Modern English*. Here we will substitute the name of *Jesus* for *love* to show that these exemplify the nature and character of Jesus.

Jesus is slow to lose patience—He looks for a way of being constructive. Jesus is not possessive: Jesus is neither anxious to impress nor does He cherish inflated ideas of His own importance. Jesus has good manners and does not pursue selfish advantage. Jesus is not touchy. Jesus does not keep account of evil or gloat over the wickedness of other people. On the contrary, Jesus is glad with all good men when truth prevails. Jesus knows no limit to His endurance, Jesus has no end to His trust, Jesus never fades in His hope. Jesus can outlast anything. Jesus is, in fact, the one thing that still stands when all else has fallen.

These are the characteristics of a person who has been conformed to the likeness of Christ Jesus. Read over these statements again in both translations and see if your way of life includes all areas of the Christ-life.

Christlike in Righteousness

Here is God the Father's testimony about Jesus and righteousness:

For to which of the angels did [Father God] ever say: "You are My Son, today I have begotten You"? And again: "I will be to Him a Father, and He shall be to Me a Son"? But when He again brings the firstborn into the world, He says: "Let all the angels of God worship Him." And of the angels He says: "Who makes His angels spirits and His ministers a flame of fire." *But to the Son* He says: "Your throne, O God, is forever and ever; a scepter of righteousness is the scepter of Your kingdom. *You have loved righteousness and hated lawlessness*; therefore God, Your God, has anointed You with the oil of gladness more than Your companions."

Hebrews 1:5–9, emphasis added

If we are going to be like Jesus, then we must develop a real love for righteousness and a real hatred for lawlessness. Then we will be anointed with the oil of gladness more than our uncommitted companions.

Biblical righteousness is simply being right with God and doing everything that is right in God's sight. We start out being a child of God by having all our sins washed away by the blood of Jesus. At the same time, we are born of God by the Holy Spirit, and God imparts His righteousness within us. His righteousness is His nature and character. In 2 Peter 1:4 the apostle Peter declares that we are made partakers of God's divine nature. We are then to grow in Christ's nature, character and the righteousness of God until we mature into the likeness of Christ Jesus.

One who has come to Christlikeness does everything that is pleasing to God and right in His sight. It is said of Enoch that he walked with God and was such an example of God's kind of man and he pleased the Lord so much that God translated him to heaven to be with Him. Evidently God had not had a mortal who He could walk and talk with since Adam and Eve in the Garden of Eden. God is still looking for righteous men and women with whom He can walk and talk, sharing His mysteries and purposes.

It would require a whole book to list all the things that are right and wrong according to God's biblical standards. Nevertheless, we will gain great favor with God like Enoch if we allow God to conform us to Christlikeness in His righteousness. (See Genesis 5:24; Hebrews 11:5; Jude 1:14–15.)

Christlike in Attitude

Jesus demonstrated the attitude of humbleness, with complete submission to the will of God. There was no self-centeredness in Jesus. His greatest passion was to do the will of His Father and to fulfill all that Father God had sent Him to earth to fulfill as a mortal man. Jesus said, "I always do those things that please the Father." When Jesus arrived at His main purpose for coming to earth as a mortal man—to die on the cross—He prayed with tears and supplication for God to deliver Him from death. But when His Father made it emphatically clear that it was His will for Him to go through the horrible humiliation and suffering of the cross, Jesus said, "Not My will but Thine be done."

A person who has attained Christlikeness does not ask God "Why me?" when asked to do something that would crucify the self-life, mortify the flesh and cause loss of relationships or possessions. As the apostle Paul said, "I will take pleasure in this process You are putting me through, for I know it is all working together for my good to be conformed to Your likeness. Therefore, I will rejoice evermore, and in all things give thanks. For all these things I'm going through are my 'friends' and 'employees' working for my conformity to Your likeness. Since my greatest passion is to be conformed to Your likeness, it is well with my soul" (see 2 Corinthians 12:10).

As the old hymn says, all that I ask is to be like Him. When you become conformed to the likeness of Christ Jesus you will have this attitude toward whatever you go through in life.

Christlike in Work

God and His Word have a very positive attitude toward physical work as well as spiritual work. The first thing God told Adam to do—after He put him in the Garden and told him not to eat of the Tree of Knowledge of Good and Evil—was go to work. Do the physical work of being a caretaker of his home—the great Garden of Eden. Taking care of the Garden would include cultivating the ground, pruning the fruit trees and grape vines, replanting in the spring the vegetable plants and the fruit of the vine, such as watermelon and cantaloupes, etc. God told Adam to do mental work by naming all the living creatures that God had created. God did not tell Adam to cut down some trees and build a little chapel and go into it and stay there and worship God all day, then come out in the evening and fellowship with Him.

You will recall that in my book *Who Am I and Why Am I Here?* I list eight reasons why God created man. Worship is number seven and fellowship is number eight. When I taught in Bible college, I had the students fill out a form and one of the questions was, "For what purpose did God create man?"

Ninety-eight percent of the students answered *worship* and/ or *fellowship*. Important as those two are, there are six purposes before them that are more personal, meaningful and beneficial to God than the last two.

The Word says that if a person does not work, he does not eat. If he is capable of work but is too lazy to work, then the Church is not obligated to make sure he has food. Jesus spent half of His life working in manual labor as a general contractor in masonry and carpentry. God worked six days creating everything for humankind's habitation on earth. He rested the seventh day and went back to work on the eighth day, working with the mankind race.

Work in its different forms is mentioned more than eight hundred times in the Bible. Work is ordained and sanctified by God. Man can give honor to God by doing excellent work. There is good natural work and good spiritual works: "They may see your good works and glorify your Father in heaven" (Matthew 5:16). The individual who comes to Christlikeness will do natural work heartily as unto the Lord. The Christ-like person will do the work of ministry and demonstrate the works of God.

Christlike in Wisdom

The following Scriptures reveal that Christlike wisdom is from above and has distinctive divine characteristics. They contrast it to so-called wisdom that is earthly, sensual and devilish. The Word says this of Lucifer:

> "You were the seal of perfection, full of wisdom and perfect in beauty. . . . You were the anointed cherub who covers. . . .

You were perfect in your ways from the day you were created, till iniquity was found in you. . . . Your heart was lifted up because of your beauty; you corrupted your wisdom for the sake of your splendor."

Ezekiel 28:12, 14–15, 17

Though Lucifer was perfect in beauty and full of wisdom, yet he corrupted his wisdom through his selfish pride. His heavenly wisdom became earthly, selfish and devilish.

I can understand how Lucifer could have become self-deceived from being so beautiful and perfect in his ways. But it is hard to grasp how he could have been deceived while being full of wisdom. Wisdom is supposed to give you the common sense to think logically and reasonably with a sane mind. Lucifer's thinking that he could take God's place as God of the universe definitely was not reasonable or of a sound mind.

Here is what the Word says about this:

Who is *wise* and understanding among you? Let him show by good conduct that his works are done in the meekness of *wisdom*. But if you have bitter envy and self-seeking in your hearts, do not boast and lie against the truth. This *wisdom* does not descend from above but is earthly, sensual, demonic. For where envy and self-seeking exist, confusion and every evil thing are there. But the *wisdom* that is from above is first *pure*, then *peaceable, gentle, willing to yield, full of mercy and good fruits, without partiality and without hypocrisy*. Now the fruit of righteousness is sown in peace by those who make peace.

James 3:13–18, emphasis added

The Phillips paraphrase of verse 18 says the "peace-makers . . . go on quietly sowing for a harvest of righteousness."

Study Proverbs 8–9 to discover all the characteristics and the nature of wisdom. There are many definitions of *wisdom* in the books of Proverbs and Ecclesiastes. Remember, the whole New Testament is a demonstration and revelation of who Jesus is. Read the Scriptures to know more about Jesus. The person who is Christlike will manifest these characteristics of wisdom.

Christlike in Faith

The gospels, especially John, describe how Jesus related to His Father. Jesus had absolute confidence that Father God always heard His prayers. When He raised Lazarus from the grave, Jesus prayed, "Father, I thank You that You have heard Me. And I know that You always hear Me" (John 11:41–42). When Jesus cursed the fig tree because it did not have any fruit on it, His disciples were amazed, because it withered and died. Jesus responded by saying,

> "Have faith in God. For assuredly, I say to you, whoever says to this mountain, 'Be removed and be cast into the sea,' and does not doubt in his heart, but believes that those things he says will be done, he will have whatever he says. Therefore I say to you, whatever things you [desire] ask when you pray, believe that you receive them, and you will have them."
>
> Mark 11:22–24

Every time Jesus did something supernatural, He conveyed to His disciples that they could do the same thing. If they would not doubt in their hearts but speak in faith and decree it to be, it would happen. Jesus even declared emphatically, "Most assuredly, I say to you, he who believes in Me, the works that I do he will do also; and greater works than these he will do, because I go to My Father" (John 14:12).

During the Dark Age of the Church, most all of the New Testament experiential truths were pushed into the future, relegated to the past or formalized into dead religious works. They kept some of the New Testament terminology but lost the transforming power that was supposed to accompany it. Jesus described that as having a form of godliness but denying the power thereof.

The Protestant movement in the 1500s delivered us from trying to be justified by the dead works of the Dark Age Church and embraced living faith that justified us and gives us a born-again experience. The Evangelical movement in the 1600s restored water baptism by immersion, personal evangelism and several other fundamental beliefs. The Holiness movement in the 1700s restored the truth that Christians can live a holy life, victorious over sin and worldliness—sanctified by grace and faith. The Divine Healing movement starting in the 1880s brought revelation regarding the truth that healing for the physical body of man was provided by the 39 stripes Jesus received, just as the blood He shed was for the cleansing of our spirit man from sin. Millions have been miraculously healed since that time. There are special gifts of healing and miracles, but there are also the miracles of believers laying hands on the sick and seeing them healed.

Since that time to the present hundreds of books have been written on the reality that the supernatural is to be a part of the ministry of every saint. All five restoration movements that have happened from 1880 till 2007 have included divine physical healing in their belief systems and practices. (See Isaiah 53:5; Matthew 10:1, 7–8; Mark 16:17–18; 1 Corinthians 12:7–11; 1 Peter 2:24.)

Jesus died on the cross and was buried, but He arose on the third day and ascended to the Father, and as He had promised, He sent the Holy Spirit on the Day of Pentecost. It was the same Holy Spirit who empowered Jesus to do miracles. If we are to be conformed to the likeness of Christ, we must come to the place where we have a relationship with Jesus just as He had with His Father. We must believe in our hearts that we can do anything He tells us to do, be anything He wants us to be, fulfill everything He commissions us to fulfill.

Some will make it to that conformity to Jesus Christ. I know I am not there yet, but I am believing for an infusion of His grace that will enable me to be able to say with the apostle Paul, "I can do all things through Christ who strengthens me." We cannot become what Christ Jesus has not called us to be, but we can be assured that we can be transformed and then conformed to His likeness with the supernatural as part of our lives and ministries.

Christlike in Holiness

Because God is holy, He demanded His only begotten Son be holy even while living as a man in a mortal body. God also demands that all of His Spirit-born children be holy. "As He who called you is holy, you also be holy in all your conduct, because it is written, 'Be holy, for I am holy'" (1 Peter 1:15–16). For a Christian, being holy is having the heart of

God and the mind of Christ. You feel as God feels about things, and you think as Christ thinks about things. You have a purified and clean heart, mind and attitude. Those who reach Christlikeness will have appropriated Christ's attitude and attributes.

"Pursue . . . holiness, without which no one will see the Lord" (Hebrews 12:14). One of the beatitudes declares that only those who have pure hearts will be able to see God (see Matthew 5:8). A pure heart and mind do not respond to the three basic sin producers—the lust of the flesh, the lust of the eyes and the pride of life.

During the 1960s when I was teaching in the Bible college, the dress styles for women began to change. The stylish length of dresses began to go up from midcalf to one to three inches above the knees. The young men came to me fussing that we needed to make the young women keep their dress hems below their knees, for when they took their seats on the platform it did not leave much to the imagination.

Accordingly, we passed a rule that the women's dresses had to touch the floor when they stood on their knees. This helped the young men to some degree, by not letting them see as much leg exposed.

But I said to them, "If the whole world of females started going naked in public, you would have to grow in the grace of God until you were able to glance at the body of a beautiful woman and not think sensuous thoughts."

Some of the young men were able to overcome by the grace of God giving them holy and pure hearts and minds that enabled them not to respond in a lustful way. It is possible, for God walked and talked with Adam and Eve in their nakedness until they ate of the forbidden fruit tree. I am sure

God did not have any improper thoughts about Eve's naked body. There will be no lust or covetousness in heaven.

Can God's will be done on earth as it is in heaven? There will be a remnant gathered from ages past until the coming of the Lord who have allowed Father God to transform their lives in whatever way necessary to work the very nature and character of Christlikeness into every fiber of their whole being—body, soul and spirit.

Christlike in Human Relationships

Our first and greatest relationship is with God. The second is fellowship with our fellow human beings. In the New Testament the apostle John talks the most frequently about human relationships. The book of Proverbs covers it the most in the Old Testament. Our greatest test in being Christlike usually comes in dealing with other people. The Bible is full of admonitions for us to love our neighbors as we love ourselves; to do unto others as we would have them do unto us. Christians are to bless those who curse us and do good to those who make our lives miserable. To be tenderhearted and forgiving of others even as Christ has forgiven us.

The apostle John speaks strongly about loving others.

Beloved, let us love one another, for love is of God; and everyone who loves is born of God and knows God. He who does not love does not know God, for God is love. In this the love of God was manifested toward us, that God has sent His only begotten Son into the world, that we might live through Him. In this is love, not that we loved God, but that He loved us and sent His Son to be the propitiation for our sins. Beloved, if God so loved us, we also ought to love one another.

1 John 4:7–11

This love is unselfish and self-sacrificing as Jesus demonstrated by being sacrificed on the cross so that others might be saved. It is such love that if you are not motivated by this God-love in everything you do, then your great works count for nothing. Chapter 9 of this book covers the blessings of forgiving others and the judgments of God for not forgiving. God also notices how we treat the needy, poor, widows and orphans.

If we are really desirous to be like Jesus, then we must move forward to face the giant (selfishness) that everyone is afraid to try to kill. If you have love for God's people and a just cause, you will go against impossible odds, winning and inspiring others to attack and fight the good fight of faith. Those who overcome and give all that they have will be greatly rewarded in this life a hundredfold and will receive in the world to come everlasting life and the privilege of being co-heirs reigning with Christ Jesus.

Christlike in Growth and Maturity

The Bible talks much about growing, adding, multiplying and increasing until we reach a certain age, stage, maturity, etc. At the same time, it talks about decreasing, subtracting and taking off. It is off with the old man and on with the new. John the Baptist said, "Jesus must increase, but I must decrease." My self-life must die more and more while my Christ-life must be alive in me more than ever before.

We must know what Jesus knows and major in what He majors in. Jesus knows He is coming again to resurrect and translate His saints, but He does not major in that. There are three statements in Scripture about "going up," but there are more than thirty statements in Scripture about "growing up." The Holy Spirit is working more on our transformation than our translation; more on our conformity to Jesus than His coming again. He wants the Church grown up before He takes it up. Jesus is held in the heavens until the restoration of the Church and the transformation of the saints (see Acts 3:21; Ephesians 4:11, 15).

The apostle Peter gives us direction on what to do to make sure we do not fail; that we make our calling and election sure; that we are successful in life and in Christ Jesus. Notice the key words emphasizing what we just discussed.

Grace and peace be multiplied to you in the knowledge of God and of Jesus our Lord, as His divine power has given to us all things that pertain to life and godliness, through the knowledge of Him who called us by glory and virtue, by which have been given to us exceedingly great and precious promises, that through these you may be partakers of the divine nature, having escaped the corruption that is in the world through lust. But also for this very reason, giving all diligence, add to your faith virtue, to virtue knowledge, to knowledge self-control, to self-control perseverance, to perseverance godliness, to godliness brotherly kindness, and to brotherly kindness love. For if these things are yours and abound, you will be neither barren nor unfruitful in the knowledge of our Lord Jesus Christ. For he who lacks these things is shortsighted, even to blindness, and has forgotten that he was cleansed from his old sins. Therefore, brethren, be even more diligent to make your call and election sure, for if you do these things you will never stumble; for so an entrance will be supplied to you abundantly into the everlasting kingdom of our Lord and Savior Jesus Christ.

2 Peter 1:2–11

An individual is born as a baby, but God's natural order is that the person not stay a baby but grow to adulthood. The Church was born on the Day of Pentecost but was designed to grow until she reached maturity and fulfilled all that God has predestined for her to fulfill.

Jesus declared, "I will *build* My Church," not just birth it. Jesus divided His ministry to the Church into five ministries and gave them to specially chosen saints. He called those gifted in the five ministries *apostles*, *prophets*, *evangelists*, *pastors* and *teachers*. Their commission is to equip the saints in their ministries in the Body of Christ and build the Body of Christ *until* the Church comes into the unity of the faith, the knowledge of the Son of God, to a perfect man—which is Christlikeness, the fullness and maturity of Christ Himself (see Ephesians 4:11–16).

The Holy Spirit is working through Christ's fivefold ministers to finalize the building of the Church in the quality and quantity that God has purposed. Most of my other books cover the restoration of the Church and what it will look like by the time Jesus returns for His Bride. My book titled *Prophetic Scriptures Yet to Be Fulfilled* covers the First Reformation, which was for the birthing and establishing of the Church; the Second Reformation, which covers the nine major restoration movements during the last five hundred years of the Church; and then introduces the Third and final

Reformation, which was launched into the Church in 2008. It reveals what the Third Reformation is to accomplish and fulfill so that the Second Coming of Christ can take place. My book prior to this one, *God's Weapons of War*, reveals that the present move of God in the Church is the Army of the Lord movement. It covers how the Church is to do corporate spiritual warfare in the nations. I have led churches in doing corporate spiritual warfare in thirty nations.

This book, *Your Highest Calling*, is written for the individual sons and daughters of God to come to maturity. I believe it covers some of the most important truths that Christians need to know to be able to live victoriously and finish well. In this book I have majored on God's purpose for conforming His foreknown and predestined ones to the image and likeness of Christ.

The key truth is understanding the Process that God is using to conform us to the likeness of His Son. I pray that the Law of Transformation and the Process for Conformity, as built around Romans 8:28–29, will be born of God in your heart. If it becomes birthed within, it will free you from confusion, condemnation, hurts, disappointments and questions you have about some of the traumas, tragedies, trials and tests that you have experienced. The truth will make you free and knock the "why" out of the mysteries of life's happenings.

Christlike in Prayer and Worship

Those who become Christlike will have a prayer life like Jesus'. Jesus prayed often, several times all night. At Bible college I taught about prayer for one semester. We discovered six different types of prayers, each to accomplish a different purpose. One was to demonstrate our dependence upon God for greater intimacy and relationship with Him. When Jesus gave all of His ministries to the fivefold ministers and the saints, He left one for Himself: making intercession for the saints (see Romans 8:34).

There are hardly any Scriptures about Jesus worshiping. They sang a psalm at the Last Supper, and in prophetic Scripture Jesus says, "In the midst of the assembly I will sing praise to You" (Hebrews 2:12). To find worship and praise, as we enjoy today, you have to go to the psalms of David. He reveals the heart of God in worship, for Scripture says, "I have found David . . . a man after My own heart" (Acts 13:22). Those who conform to Christlikeness will be enthusiastic praisers and worshipers of Jesus Christ.

Christlike in the "10 M's"

In the late 1970s I started teaching and activating Christians into the prophetic ministry. In the early 1980s I started the School of the Prophets for teaching, activating and training young men and women to be ministers. Those who were called to be prophets we trained to be biblically sound, with a proper character and attitude. The rest we taught how to be true to whatever fivefold ministry they were called, but also to add the prophetic into their ministries.

To make sure they all received well-rounded and balanced teaching, I developed what I called the "10 M's." It was called that because all the descriptive words used start with the letter *M*. For years I only had them listed in teaching outlines. In 1990 I listed them on page 155 of my newly published book, *Prophets and the Prophetic Movement*. The next year, 1991, I published *Prophets, Pitfalls, and Principles*. The "10 M's" were listed on page 66 and were followed by 24 pages of teaching about them. They were listed again in my twelfth book called *How Can These Things Be?*

The "10 M's" are designed to teach ministers (I use the term *manhood* to describe the human race; these apply equally to men and women) how to maintain their ministry in purity and balance while they are moving to maturity. They are also used to evaluate and determine true and false ministers.

At CIAN we have discussed much about how many M's have to be out of order before a person would be classified as a false minister. Some of the M's are more serious than others. We dismissed one of our ministers because his problem was Manners, but there were also root problems of Maturity and Motive. He had the greatest healing ministry of anyone on the team that I sent to a particular nation. But he was rude, demanding, ill-mannered and discourteous to waiters, receptionists, the driver and some of his fellow ministers. We counseled with him several times, but he did not respond with the heavenly wisdom that is gentle, easy to be entreated and teachable. He could not and would not acknowledge his wrong attitude and actions. We had to dismiss him from being an ordained minister with Christian International Apostolic Network.

I want to list these "10 M's" at the close of this chapter because if God sees that you are weak in any of these, He will assign the Holy Spirit to begin His transforming and conforming Process until the weakness is a strength. One minister told me that he had no need to be concerned about them for he was in good shape in all except for one of them (which was one of the more serious ones).

I said, "Brother, let me give you an illustration, and then you tell me if you need to be concerned about that one, okay?"

He agreed, so I said, "I want you to visualize that you are hanging over a three-thousand-foot cliff, and the only thing holding you is a metal chain with ten links. Nine of them are in good shape, but one is getting paper-thin in one area and beginning to stretch a little. Are you going to be bragging about how great and strong those nine links are and ignore the one that is about to break? Do you remember the old saying that a chain is only as strong as its weakest link?"

The Process Will Continue

Those whom Father God has chosen to co-labor with Christ Jesus throughout eternity are destined to be taken through the Law of Transformation and the Process for Conformity. This will be repeated again and again in our lifetimes until we are one hundred percent living His Christlike nature, His character in body, soul and spirit. The apostle Paul said in his letter to the Philippians that he was not sure he had attained unto the status of Christlikeness (see Philippians 3:12–14). But in Galatians 2:20 he described what Christlikeness is like: "I have been crucified with Christ; it is no longer I who live, but Christ lives in me; and the life which I now live in the flesh I live by faith in the Son of God, who loved me and gave Himself for me."

Paul wrote to the Colossian Christians to set their minds, desires and emotions on heavenly things more than their own self-desires, "for you died, and your life is hidden with Christ in God. When Christ *who is our life* appears, then you also will appear with Him in glory [Christlikeness]" (Colossians 3:3–4, emphasis added). Too many Christians accept Jesus only as their Savior to deliver them from sin and to save them from going to the fiery place called hell. He is their fire escape! Some accept Christ Jesus as deliverer, healer, baptizer and other roles that bless them. But very few die completely to self and allow Christ to become their whole lives, becoming more inclined to please Jesus than themselves.

Do we serve God just for what He can do for us? Is most of our prayer communication with Him trying to get Him to do more for us? How many of our requests are for ways and means that we can serve Jesus better, live His life more fully and manifest who Jesus is to the world; that we can let our lights so shine that others will glorify God because of the Christ-life they see manifested through us?

I am fairly sure that you would not be reading this book if you did not have a deep desire to be more like Jesus. You appreciate so much what Jesus has done for you that your passion is to do everything in your ability to surrender everything to Him. You are willing not only to allow but also to welcome whatever you must go through in life for the Law of Transformation and the Process for Conformity to bring you to Christlikeness.

Romans 8:28–29 will now become more than a revelation; it will be a passion and working reality in your life. Your petition before God will be what Paul declared and prayed: "I count all things loss that I may know Jesus and the fellowship of His sufferings—that I may be like Him" (see Philippians 3:7–10).

We shall be like Him!

"And everyone who has this hope in Him purifies himself, just as [Jesus] is pure" (1 John 3:3).

ACKNOWLEDGMENT & PETITION

Father God, I have this hope in me to be just as Jesus is. The way I am purifying myself is to allow Your Holy Spirit to continue the conforming Process in me until I have reached complete Christlikeness in every area of my life and total being. May my every thought and action be according to Your Word, will, way and wisdom. May every truth in this book that begins in my heart as revelation, advance to living reality in me. The time will come when I will be standing in Your literal presence, and I want to hear You say, "Welcome home, child. You have fought a good fight of faith and fulfilled all the things I commissioned you to fulfill for Me. You allowed Me to transform you to be like My Son, Jesus. Now join Us with all the heroes of faith as we embark upon our eternal ministry together forever." Amen—so be it!

10 M's

*For Maturing and Maintaining Manhood
and Ministry, and Determining Prophetic
Ministers' True/False Status*

---

1. MANHOOD

Genesis 1:26–27	God makes a man before manifesting mighty ministry
Romans 8:29	Man—apart from position, message or ministry
Hebrews 2:6, 10	"Per-son-al-ity"—evaluating person not performance
1 Timothy 2:5	Jesus—manhood 30 years; ministry 3½; 10 to 1 ratio

2. MINISTRY

2 Corinthians 6:3	No offense to ministry; 1 Corinthians 2:4–5—power and demonstration
Matthew 7:15–21	By their fruits you shall know them—anointing, results
Deuteronomy 18:22	Prophecies or preaching productive—proven, pure, positive

3. MESSAGE

Ephesians 4:15	Speak the truth in love, present-truth and life giving
1 Timothy 4:2	Message balanced, scriptural, doctrinally and spiritually right
Mark 16:20	God confirms His Word—not person, pride or reputation

4. MATURITY

James 3:17	Attitude right, mature in human relations, heavenly wisdom
Galatians 5:22	Fruit of Spirit, Christlike character, dependable, steadfast, Hebrews 5:14
1 Corinthians 13	Not childish, biblically knowledgeable and mature—not a novice

5. MARRIAGE

1 Timothy 3:2, 5	Scripturally in order, personal family vs. God's family
1 Peter 3:1, 7	Priorities straight—God first, spouse, family and ministry
Ephesians 5:22–23	Marriage to exemplify relationship of Christ and His Church

6. METHODS

Titus 1:16	Rigidly righteous, ethical, honest, integrity—upright
Romans 1:18	Not manipulating or deceptive, does not speak "evangelistically"
Romans 3:7–8	Good end results do not justify unscriptural methods

7. MANNERS

Titus 1:7; 3:1–2	Unselfish, polite, kind, gentleman or lady, discreet
Ephesians 4:29; 5:4	Proper speech and communication in words and mannerisms

8. MONEY

1 Timothy 3:8 AMPC	"Craving wealth and resorting to ignoble and dishonest methods"
1 Timothy 6:5–17	Luke 12:15—Love of money and materialism destroys (e.g., Achan)

9. MORALITY

1 Corinthians 6:9–18	Virtuous, pure and proper relationships, Colossians 3:5
Ephesians 5:3	Biblical sexual purity in attitude and action, 1 Corinthians 5:11
Matthew 5:28	Wrong thoughts with desire to do—without opportunity to act

10. MOTIVE

Matthew 6:1	To serve or to be seen? Fulfill personal drive or God's desire?
1 Corinthians 16:15	True motivation? To minister or to be a minister?
Proverbs 16:2	To herald the truth or just to be heard by man?
1 Corinthians 13:1–3	Motivated by God's love or lust for power, fame, name, etc.?

When God calls a man or woman to be a prophet, destined to have a major impact upon the Church, the calling brings with it much preparation, learning, experience and great tests. In 1950, fifteen-year-old **Bill Hamon** was living on his parents' farm with his father, mother, two brothers and two sisters, none of whom was churchgoing. In July of that year, Bill attended a three-week revival at a brush arbor meeting about two miles from his house. Riding his horse to the meetings every night, he went to the altar on his sixteenth birthday and received Jesus Christ as his Savior. He was filled with the Holy Spirit and prayed for 45 minutes in his Spirit language. (The complete story is told in the preface to his book *Prophets and Personal Prophecy*, written by his wife, Evelyn Yvonne Hamon. It is also in his book *The Day of the Saints*.)

Over the next thirty years, Bishop Hamon was trained through attending Bible college, pastoring, evangelizing, teaching at a Bible college and then establishing Christian International School of Theology. In his second thirty-plus years, he has built the Christian International Ministries Network, which now has an apostolic network of more than five thousand ministers. During Bishop Hamon's 66 years of ministry, he has traveled to seventy nations and has in recent years led thirty of those nations in corporate warfare.

Recognized as the father of the modern Prophetic movement, Bishop Hamon has pioneered and grown in prophetic ministry, personally prophesying to more than fifty thousand individuals, ranging from presidents of nations to babies in their mothers' arms. At the same time, he has endured major tests that were heartbreaking, mind-blowing and world-shaking, yet also part of the making of a major restoration prophet.

"It takes years to develop the '10 M's' (manhood, ministry, message, maturity, marriage, methods, manners, money, morality and motive) that are essential to developing in and maintaining ministry," Bishop Hamon says. "It is good to desire to do great things for God; you must, however, understand that the greater the calling, the greater the testing and purifying. I fully agree with Apostle Paul's declaration in Romans 8:18 [KJV]: 'For I reckon that the sufferings [tests and trials] of this present time are not worthy to be compared with the glory [co-laboring with Christ] which shall be revealed in [and through] us.' And Galatians 6:9 NIV: 'At the proper time we will reap a harvest if we do not give up.' Amen."

In this book, Dr. Bill Hamon does not emphasize his great accomplishments but the processes we have to go through to fulfill God's highest calling for our lives. He has been interviewed several times on the national Christian television networks. Dr. Hamon has written fourteen books; his wife, Evelyn, three; and his three children, seven.

At age 21, while pastoring a church, Bishop Hamon married his wife, Evelyn. They have three children (Tim, Tom and Sherilyn), eleven grandchildren and, as of this writing, eighteen great-grandchildren. All three of Bishop Hamon's children are ordained ministers serving in leadership roles at Christian International. In September 2014 Bishop Hamon's wife finished her race and ascended to heaven, where we all shall join her someday.

Christian International

Christian International Apostolic Network (CIAN) and Christian International Global Network (CIGN)

The CIAN/CIGN mandate is to restore the fivefold ministry to the Body of Christ and to provide relationship and affiliation.

Christian International School Prophets (CISP)

CISP provides teaching, training and activating in prophetic and apostolic ministry.

Christian International Equipping Network (CIEN)

CIEN serves apostolic and prophetic training centers around the world.

CI Culture Influencers (CICI)

CICI equips and commissions those called to the marketplace.

Manual for Ministering Spiritual Gifts

This seminar combines sound biblical truth with CI's primary role of activating others. Over 500,000 have been trained and activated.

Annual International Gathering of Apostles and Prophets (IGAP)

For 32 years, believers have gathered to receive global direction from God through His modern-day apostles and prophets.

Watchman Leadership Summit (WLS)

WLS is the first and only national prophetic watchman/warfare gathering of its kind.

www.christianinternational.com

More from Dr. Bill Hamon

With the end times upon us, renowned prophetic leader Dr. Bill Hamon calls the Church to a higher level of warfare: corporate spiritual warfare. Here he shows how the Church can work in unity, identifies the weapons available for this new fight and reveals a battle plan for destroying the works of the devil and advancing God's Kingdom.

God's Weapons of War